WOMEN'S STUDIES

THE BASICS

Women's Studies: The Basics is an accessible introduction to the ever-expanding and increasingly relevant field of studies focused on women. Tracing the history of the discipline from its origins, this text sets out the main agendas of women's studies and feminism, exploring the global development of the subject over time, and highlighting its relevance in the contemporary world. Reflecting the diversity of the field, core themes include:

- the interdisciplinary nature of women's studies
- core feminist theories and the feminist agenda
- issues of intersectionality: women, race, class, and gender
- women, sexuality, and the body.

Providing a firm foundation for all those new to the subject, this book is valuable reading for undergraduates and postgraduates majoring in women's studies and gender studies, and all those in related disciplines seeking a helpful overview for women-centred, subject-specific courses.

Bonnie G. Smith is Board ... ry and Women's Studies at Rutger ... :d widely on the subjects of wor ... d gender.

D1059293

The Basics

WOMEN'S STUDIES

THE BASICS

Bonnie G. Smith

Routledge
Taylor & Francis Group

LONDON AND NEW YORK

First published 2013
by Routledge
2 Park Square, Milton Park, Abingdon, Oxon OX14 4RN

Simultaneously published in the USA and Canada
by Routledge
711 Third Avenue, New York, NY 10017

Routledge is an imprint of the Taylor & Francis Group, an informa business

© 2013 Bonnie G. Smith

British Library Cataloguing in Publication Data
A catalogue record for this book is available from the British Library

Library of Congress Cataloging in Publication Data
Smith, Bonnie G., 1940-
Women's studies : the basics / Bonnie G. Smith.
p. cm. – (The basics)
1. Women's studies. I. Title.
HQ1180.S58 2013
305.4 – dc23
2012029098

ISBN: 978-0-415-60941-8 (hbk)
ISBN: 978-0-415-60944-9 (pbk)
ISBN: 978-0-203-07102-1 (ebk)

Typeset in Bembo
by Taylor & Francis Books

Printed and bound by CPI Group (UK) Ltd, Croydon, CR0 4YY

CONTENTS

ACKNOWLEDGMENTS

I would like to thank my colleagues in Women's Studies and Women's History at Rutgers University for their scholarship and inspiring examples as teachers, both of which this book draws on extensively. Sincere thanks as well to Nova Robinson for her research on Middle Eastern women's global networks and for her help in the final preparation of the book for publication.

THE INVENTION OF WOMEN'S STUDIES

Women's Studies is arguably the most revolutionary new field of intellectual inquiry of our current age. In its simplest form, Women's Studies brings all of women's experience under the scholarly microscope, subjecting it to the most advanced scientific methods available in the university. Researchers dig up facts and develop insights about that experience and then teachers and students look at the findings coming from an array of disciplines, processing and often perfecting them. Women's Studies programs include almost every perspective—from the natural sciences to the social sciences, from law to the arts. This breadth makes Women's Studies the most wide-ranging of academic fields. Its rich diversity provides the judgments, research, and energy of a broad group of scholars and students to advance the discipline.

Women's Studies is a global undertaking. It began almost simultaneously around the world. Ewha University in Seoul, South Korea began its first Women's Studies program in 1977. In the United States, Cornell University and California State University, San Diego, began Women's Studies programs in 1969; more generally in the United States, Women's Studies grew from several courses in individual universities across the country in the late 1960s to more than 600 degree-granting majors and programs today. India established vigorous Women's Studies research in the early 1970s and became one of the most active countries in the world to investigate women's experience and thought. Even this phenomenal growth hardly captures the excitement that continues to motivate those in Women's Studies.

The founding of Women's Studies was full of drama, as the positive energy of the first students and teachers met with disapproval from male administrators, male authors, and male leaders of established departments in the West. Some governments pushed for Women's Studies programs as part of generally moving their countries forward, while the decades of the 1970s and 1980s saw women at the grassroots fighting established dictators. It was also a time when celebrated Western intellectuals in sociobiology and anthropology were asserting women's biological and intellectual inferiority as scientific fact and pointing, in contrast, to the risk-taking and intellectual originality of men. Women's Studies was a fad, other naysayers claimed, and one without the slightest intellectual merit. The field was simply gynecological politics, according to still others. Yet, after several millennia of reflection on human existence and the world of nature that excluded women and that saw them as unworthy of consideration, the field of Women's Studies inquiry not only emerged to recharge the human mind at the time but continues on its innovative path today.

WOMEN'S STUDIES: WHAT IS IT?

Women's Studies is not exactly new. Despite public and professional neglect, for centuries there have been histories of women, anthologies of women's literary writing, and statistical and sociological studies of such topics as the working conditions of women and the organization of family life. The African oral history tradition had long celebrated noble, accomplished women. Early written studies were mostly produced by amateurs in the eighteenth and nineteenth century, who often found appreciative women readers and even received praise from male commentators. Yet not everyone applauded. Consider the case of Lucy Maynard Salmon, who taught an early form of Women's Studies at Vassar College until the 1920s. Salmon had trained with the great scholars of her day, including Woodrow Wilson, who would become US president in 1913. Salmon's master's thesis on the appointing powers of American presidents won a national prize. After that, however, approval from the professionals declined as she began writing about domestic service, kitchens, cookbooks, and outdoor museums that displayed farmhouses and household tools. She was interdisciplinary and used methods that historians, art historians, sociologists, and others now blend today in their study of women, and she is credited by them for such innovative techniques as "reading the vernacular landscape." At the time, however, young male teachers tried to get her fired from her post as department chair even as others began adopting some of her methods. Salmon was an unsung pioneer in Women's Studies, but one who stubbornly continued her inspiring investigations and the pursuit of methodological creativity.

In the late 1960s, some half a century after Salmon's retirement, individual courses took shape in Canada, Great Britain, the United States, India, and elsewhere around the world to investigate women's literature, history, and psychology, and to look at them through the lens of the professional lens of sociology, economics, and politics. Scholars probed their disciplines for evidence on women and came up with astonishing material such as criminal and work records, diaries and account books, reports on fertility, health, and activism. What was most astonishing is that disciplines had almost unanimously claimed no such evidence existed and that studies of women in most fields were impossible because traces of their existence simply did not exist. We know the outcome: essays, anthologies, monographs, novels, and ultimately reference works came rolling off the presses; databases and online bibliographies came into being; encyclopedias and biographical dictionaries produced millions of words and multiple volumes, all of them testifying to the infinite amount of facts, works of art, writing, scientific material, and philosophical thought by women. Hundreds of thousands of books sold, and within a few years Women's Studies was thriving because of these findings, the efforts of researchers, and governmental interest in women's issues, and within the growing number of individual courses about women.

Almost immediately, the new Women's Studies curriculum of the 1970s galvanized the teaching of these courses and fired the individual investigations of scholars in individual disciplines to mainstream this new knowledge—that is, to add it to the content of regular courses. These were astonishing to all who participated in opening the floodgates of knowledge or who simply watched in amazement from the sidelines. At the beginning, Women's Studies came to offer a cafeteria-like array of disciplinary investigations of the past and present conditions under which women experienced, acted, and reflected upon the world. Initially, the field mounted courses in women in the arts, the sociology of women and sex roles, women in politics, and the history of women—to name a few of the offerings. Such courses were revolutionary simply because they explicitly brought the study of women into an academic curriculum that was almost exclusively about men. There came to be more to the field of Women's Studies, however, than this initial scholarly focus on women—in fact, much, much more. This book presents some of yesterday's and many of today's concerns and achievements.

Created as a comprehensive field, programs in Women's Studies attract tens of thousands of students worldwide, and these students come from every conceivable discipline. In my own Women's Studies courses, women and men from psychology, social work, education, engineering, the sciences, and literature make the classroom a lively place as they share expertise and debate ideas with other students from history, the arts, and politics, all sharing wildly different points of view. From the beginning Women's Studies engaged the entire university population. It usually brought in those who were the most intellectually adventurous, whether the course took place in Seoul, South Korea or Los Angeles, US. In short, Women's Studies is a global scholarly enterprise with sparks of energy crossing the disciplines and uniting communities of students and teachers. All this makes Women's Studies a vastly exciting and innovative program of study.

It is hard to recapture the ignorance of women's achievements that existed in those days when Women's Studies was founded. Many of us, for example, could not name five notable women from the past or five major women authors. We were utterly ignorant of women's major role in activism—whether political or economic. For all its enthusiasm and adventurousness today, Women's Studies has a very short history in the university: the 1970s was its "age of discovery." Whereas some fields of study such as philosophy go back centuries for almost as long as there has been education, it was only recently that Women's Studies programs came into being as coherent programs of inquiry aiming to fill a massive lacuna. Often they began with experts in history and literature, who reeducated themselves to investigate women. Sometimes these pioneers team-taught to bring a comparative perspective to their initial study of women. They looked for exemplary and forgotten women writers or women actors in historical events such as revolutions and strikes. Women's Studies also focused on social scientific investigation of women in the workforce or the underground economy or women in political parties—but again, with many instructors newly creating their own expertise. The idea behind social scientific investigation was to uncover structures, create models, or to discover the ways in which social roles operated and were created. Ignorance among academics on issues such as gender inequity in the workforce was phenomenal—although women in trade unions were all too aware. Behind such investigations there was often an urgency to remedy what was seen as discrimination and the "oppression" of women through fact-finding and by reorienting entire disciplines.

Over the decades, Women's Studies has changed from an initial cluster of fledgling courses springing up in a few colleges and universities to populous programs with majors and graduate curricula. Whereas Women's Studies started in undergraduate education, its findings came to enter elementary and high schools, transforming the curriculum. Feminists criticized the ordinary curricula in schools for the total lack of information on women. It also criticized schools for fostering traditional sex roles, which gave young girls the idea that they only had one course in their lives: to be a wife and mother. Women's Studies provided a variety of options, especially when it showed the many contributions that women had made to society and the many ways in which they had made those contributions. Women's Studies investigations also gave hard evidence of the bias towards boys and young men in education. For example, they received more feedback when they talked in school and were said to be "brilliant," whereas girls and young women were characterized as "hard-working." Additional scholarship by Women's Studies researchers in the 1970s showed that in schools, an essay with a boy's name attached to it consistently received a higher grade than an identical essay with a girl's name attached. Awareness of early Women's Studies findings at all levels of education led to attempts to even the playing field for girls and young women as they progressed through the curriculum. Women's Studies made the 1970s an eye-opening time for everyone concerned with fairness, citizenship, and equal opportunity.

Along the way, Women's Studies itself changed in its content and even its personnel, as we will see in the chapters that follow. Soon after cobbling together a curriculum of individual courses from the disciplines, Women's Studies brought the various forms of inquiry under one umbrella and explicitly asked that the individual forms of inquiry consider working in tandem with the others. From a cluster of courses, Women's Studies became an international phenomenon with journals published and read internationally and with a subject matter in constant evolution. From a program that sometimes did not want male students, it found itself engaging women and men alike in classrooms and in research. It branched out to adult education courses and to technical, law, and business schools. It embraced the study of not just women but of gender. Finally, in some cases Women's Studies has changed its name and identity over the decades, going from Women's Studies to Women's and Gender Studies and sometimes becoming Gender Studies, Feminist Studies, Gender and Sexuality Studies, or simply Sexuality Studies. Women's Studies multiplied and became plural, highlighting variety in national and international meetings and associations. It is this evolving identity and plurality of practices and ideas that will be traced in the chapters of this book.

FEMINIST ROOTS OF WOMEN'S STUDIES: A BRIEF LOOK BACK

As we may know, the late 1960s and 1970s in the West were the heyday of what is sometimes called "second wave feminism," when there was noisy activism around the world for equal pay, control of women's reproduction, an end to violence against women, and women's under-representation in politics and public affairs as elected officials. Women also wanted access to good jobs and an end to discrimination in the workforce. Many countries were concerned with women's poverty, brutalization in the household, and sexual abuse not only of women but of girls and boys. This list of concerns was long, and the activism earnest and sincere. In some cases, the problems were so glaring that governments found themselves forced to pay attention and even change policies both to protect and to advance the well-being of women.

Before this activism came the "first feminist wave," which occurred in the nineteenth and early twentieth centuries when women around the world organized to gain basic rights such as the right to own property (including the wages they earned), to receive an education, to appear as witnesses in court, to bring lawsuits against aggressors, and to have the same political rights as men, such as the vote. During the "first wave," many women became avid readers of their own histories and of novels and they participated in clubs, discussion groups, and politics. Women in Egypt, India, and other colonized countries sought reforms not only for their own sake but to show that their countries were as modern as the imperial powers because of the push for women's rights. In 1905, a Bengali woman, Rokeya Sakhawat Hossain, wrote a short story, "Sultana's Dream", describing how very advanced her country would be if women ruled: gone was deadly warfare. Instead the women rulers of "Ladyland" defeated the nation's enemies by harnessing the sun's powers to drive them back; in Hossain's world there was technological efficiency and, because of it, harmonious rule. Many men in nationalist movements, including Hossain's husband, supported women's efforts because they too saw an improved status of women as making an important statement about the nation's fitness for self-rule.

In the long run, World War I (1914–18) brought the vote to many women in the West (though not in populous European states such as Italy and France). After 1945, full independence for countries such as Vietnam and Egypt, where women had played major activist roles in anti-imperialist movements, resulted in few specific advances for women when that independence from colonial rule came. The goal of independence meant everything—including a sense of belonging—and it took energy and funds to nation-build. For many women, the goal of equality was a distant dream and they contented themselves with freedom. Likewise, in the West, the vote hardly brought permanent improvements in conditions for women. Instead, "first wave feminism" seemed to wane as a public phenomenon around the world even as union women and civil service workers kept agitating for fair wages in the 1940s and 1950s and gay and lesbian activists lobbied quietly for basic human rights.

Nonetheless, for the field of Women's Studies there was consistent movement below the surface, accompanying these waves of activism and even flourishing after they ebbed. Research and writing about women's literature and women's history continued, and "liberated" women around the world loved reading such works in translation as John Stuart Mill's *On the Subjection of Women*, which boldly advocated women's equality and rights. There was far more cross-border sharing of feminist impulses: the greatest global theatrical production was the Norwegian playwright Henrik Ibsen's *A Doll's House* (1879), which sparked lively debate in Japan, China, and many other countries. *A Doll's House* tells the story of a respectable middle-class woman who leaves her husband when he shows no trust in her. Leaving her children, she decides to create an educated, responsible life for herself—a decision that shocked many audiences but that galvanized women to demand respect, independence, and jobs to support themselves. But women's publishing houses, news-letters and journals, and intensive research were as, if not more, important than these writings by male luminaries.

In the early twentieth century popular books by or about women became globally important, even though women's literacy remained low in many places. In 1926, Arthur Waley published a translation of Lady Murasaki's *Tale of Genji*, an eleventh-century classic of men, women, and court life in Japan. American author Pearl Buck's *The Good Earth* (1931) was translated into more than 30 languages, while Chinese novelist Pa Chin's *Family*—filled with oppressed women characters—was equally read worldwide. All of these portrayed the condition and activities of women, and none more vividly than *Family*, with its scenes of male domination and such abuse of women that it drove some of them to suicide. The history of women also survived the waning of feminism, although there were few women working in universities or doing work that gained them professional advancement. Working women and heroic women alike filled the pages of good books. There were, most importantly, women's periodicals around the world that published researched articles on the history, art, and general culture of women as well as statistics on their status in the economy and society. However, even magazines for housewives showed women being informed mothers and rational household managers—that is, "new" or "modern" women. These magazines also reported the research on women published by government and scientific agencies, including statistical ones, that provided detailed assessments of women's con-dition in society and their health and well-being. This material later became crucial for those involved in Women's Studies. In addition, during the "first wave," women actively set up museums that included material objects from women's everyday lives. So even as some women lobbied against apartheid in South Africa and colonialism in India, others were so inspired by the activism that they simultaneously laid the building blocks for the later development of Women's Studies around the world.

WOMEN'S STUDIES AND THE UNIVERSITY

Although "first wave" feminism helped some women enter higher education and become professionals in the social sciences, history, and literature, their numbers were small. When the "second wave" of women's activism began in the 1960s, a new emphasis on education was already taking place, as societies became "post-industrial," that is, breakthroughs in science and technology showed the need for a knowledge-based society. In many countries manufacturing was giving way to the "service sector," where jobs in such fields as health care, legal services, engineering, and social work were surpassing those in heavy industry. As a result new universities and technical schools sprang up overnight and existing universities expanded both in numbers of students and in the variety of their offerings. One accomplishment of the "second wave" was the mounting of a clear and surprisingly successful assault on the male domination of higher education, even as it engaged in this expansion. "Women's Studies grew out of the recognition of the gross inequities in women's lived realities," one South Korean researcher explained, "and through an accumulation of academic knowledge from across the disciplines exploring these problems" (Huh Ra-keum 2005: 14). From the 1970s onwards, the number of women students in universities slowly began outnumbering that of men. Some critics charged that such statistics showed the neglect of men and boys and the dis-crimination they—not women—faced. The truth of the matter was that women then and today understand that they need to get a uni-versity diploma simply to match the wages of a man who has graduated from high school.

Male domination of higher education continues, but the presence of women as professors has made for change. It's not that there were no women professors before the "second wave" and the creation of

Women's Studies. Women professors had served in universities for centuries, for example as professors of chemistry and math in eighteenth-century Italy. The important point is that Women's Studies and the feminist movement changed the consciousness of many women and men in academe to recognize the vast problem of discrimination in education. This discrimination existed in the number, salaries, and status of women in universities. There was also a laser-like focus on the consistent privileging of men in the curriculum and classroom more generally. Transformation was in the air then, and it remains in the air today because of the consciousness awakened by Women's Studies and its feminist advocates.

Women's Studies programs have been fertile and spawned many offspring. There are now centers for women's leadership, women in politics, the study of sexuality, queer and lesbian studies, women and race, and many others. Women's research centers also flourish and many of these reach out to within and outside of regions. There are co-operative ventures for publishing in the East Asian region, for example, that came out of Women's Studies. Many of these have included programs for global cooperation: for example, Rutgers University houses a Center for Women's Global Leadership, from which programs with worldwide resonance and to which ideas from women around the globe flow. Such offshoots of Women's Studies add to the changing profile of the university.

WOMEN'S STUDIES GROWS FROM KNOWLEDGE FROM OUTSIDE THE ACADEMY

Women's Studies was born within or grew alongside the women's movement, and it began with a fruitful interaction between amateurs outside the academy and professionals within it. Those in universities were uninstructed about the study of women in psychology, sociology, history, or the humanities and the arts. Outside the academy, among the general public of women, there were activists founding magazines such as *Ms.*, publishing about women in the women's press, and even founding their own feminist publishing houses such as the Feminist Press in New York or the Des Femmes press in Paris. These institutions sponsored the work of freelance writers and researchers, on which scholars began building a field of Women's Studies. Soon university and trade presses alike saw that there was a demand for books to read as part of one's everyday life or to use as courses. Women filmmakers and those in television were also active at the birth of Women's Studies. In Europe, for example, there were dozens of well-received films by directors such as the German Lina Wertmüller. The US artist Judy Chicago composed *The Dinner Party*— an installation celebrating the great women of the past, a sample of whom Chicago grouped around a large triangular table. Knowledge about and portrayals of women became big business, even as academics drew on the works of the public at large for some of its material.

Finally, Women's Studies and the centers associated with them attracted numerous independent scholars—researchers who for one reason or another did not hold positions in the university. These scholars threw and continue to throw their considerable energy into the many projects that Women's Studies now comprises. "Non-traditional" students such as those who had interrupted their studies to raise a family or find a job also found a place in Women's Studies and added their vitality to these programs. The presence of both groups added diversity of perspective and brought enormous force to the research and community-building side of Women's Studies. The world of knowledge and ideas opened up to women young and old.

CHANGING THE CLASSROOM AS PART OF CHANGING THE UNIVERSITY—FIRST STEPS

Women's Studies began at a time of social change and activism, and many movements pointed to the need for reform in colleges and universities. They were out of touch, students loudly chanted on streets around the world in the 1960s. Women's Studies, many believed, would make universities more relevant by offering courses that had direct meaning in young people's lives. This program, it was argued, would attract people to the university who had thought the teaching of Plato or poetry out of touch with the need for practical subjects. Learning how to combat violence against women or to protect the rights of children, women prisoners, and the female poor as taught in Women's Studies, would open jobs up to women who were generally shut out of positions of authority in the welfare state. Women's Studies has opened opportunity to women.

The university itself began to change in important ways when it introduced Women's Studies. For one thing, more women students came to attend universities and found the curriculum relevant, even exciting. At the time, as mentioned, the wage of a woman with a college degree was below that of a man with no college education or even without a high school diploma. By the early twenty-first century, when women generally composed more than half the college population, the need for a university degree remained as important as ever: women with such a degree now earned the equivalent of a male high school graduate's salary but not more. So the slight improvement marked progress. Women's Studies took the credit for that progress, because it offered an array of courses attractive to women students and provided them with a background that could bring them jobs in social work, psychology, technical fields such as reproductive counseling, and an array of other positions. For the first time it made the university female-friendly.

Women's Studies also led the way in changing the classroom. In the first place it brought new knowledge to the university. Whereas amateurs had been the main group to study and write seriously about women, professional expertise came to the fore and reworked what students would learn. Valuing information about women and appreciating the contributions of women in the class-room marked a drastic alteration in intellectual hierarchies. Male and female students alike became able to challenge sexist clichés and they actually did so, as probably every Women's Studies professor will attest. They had facts at their fingertips and women in particular gained a newfound confidence. The simple phenomenon of women—whether student or professor— speaking authoritatively in what was a male space marked a dramatic change in the classroom and the university. Simultaneously, the functioning of classrooms changed to value student voices more generally and to question the droning voice of a professor reading from frayed and faded notes. Informed participation, by everyone for all, flourished along with the expansion of opportunity for women to learn. Creativity thrived.

The university changed intellectually and also in terms of gender representation on the faculty and in the student body. The com-bined influence of feminist activism and Women's Studies lobbying brought more women onto both the permanent and part-time faculties and boosted the percentage of women among students. Gradually some women scholars involved in Women's Studies moved up the ranks to become high-level administrators such as university deans, chancellors, vice-presidents, and even presidents. This advance occurred in every type of institution of higher education—from community colleges to the Ivy League, and beyond. Whereas once a woman scholar might be dean of a woman's college (but rarely its president), in the twenty-first century women head major research institutions. Even though the level of women's advancement to the ranks of full or chaired professor remains low even today, there is vastly more potential than existed a century earlier.

Indications remained that despite the growth of Women's Studies programs, which many had first seen as a fad with the hope that it would disappear, there was still a powerful gender hierarchy at work. The status of Women's Studies in the 1970s and 1980s and even down to the present has remained an inferior one. Because Women's Studies is about a less well-considered social group—women—its status in the university is generally lower than that of other fields. Here's an example: one of my favorite colleagues some 30 years ago commiserated over the inferior nature of Women's Studies teaching and writing. "It must be difficult," he said soberly, "working in a field where all the books are so poor in quality." He worked in early modern history, and went on, "In my own field, a brilliant book is published almost every day." This kind person had most likely never read a book in Women's Studies or women's history, for that matter, but there was in those days and even today the conviction that any study of women had to be less well written, less well researched, and less important than books about men. This is not because Women's Studies actually *is* less important or because its books actually *are* less well crafted and researched, but because women themselves still receive lower pay and fewer social benefits and are still held in lower esteem than men. These values shape the university and the ranking of the disciplines within the curriculum. Women's Studies helped improve the climate to some extent but has not yet perfected it. There remains more to do, as will be discussed in the final chapter.

WHAT IS A WOMAN? AND OTHER EARLY QUESTIONS

In the first days of Women's Studies, several issues were key to laying foundations and shaping debates. They have resonated ever since, so we need to understand them even though they are not front-burner concerns today. The first was posed in Simone de Beauvoir's *The Second Sex* (1949), arguably the most influential book about women written in the twentieth century. Translated and read around the world, *The Second Sex* asked "What is a woman?" No one, the author claimed, would ever ask a similar question about men, nor would anyone really be puzzled about men's wants and desires. That was because men were taken to be the norm, the unquestioned human type, the universal category by which all else was measured. In contrast, women were the non-norm, the opposite and the Other.

Simone de Beauvoir was a first-class French philosopher, and she lived at the center of a well-known philosophical circle of existentialists. This philosophical school claimed that biological life in itself was not true existence but merely a natural or biological condition. Existence was something one chose and acted upon in order to create freedom. Men, de Beauvoir claimed, lived out such an existence based on choice and action. Women, as the other, lived in an unfree state, following the dictates of nature to reproduce. Additionally, women made no rational choices but rather lived as the "Other" by following the notions men had of them and all the rules and regulations for female life that society constructed. The "Other" as a concept became foundational to early Women's Studies and other fields such as post-colonial and cultural studies. It has only grown in importance, while continuing to evolve, as we shall see in later chapters.

Betty Friedan's *The Feminine Mystique* (1963) picked up on de Beauvoir's question. It described the dwindling intelligence of women who stayed at home to be housewives and mothers. Her contention that middle-class women's IQs actually dropped over their life course in the home was based on interviews with her college classmates and on statistical studies done of similar women. Moreover, Friedan claimed, women who should have led sparkling lives of creativity that enhanced society, questioned the banality of their existence: "Is this all?" she found them repeatedly asking. A woman was a trapped housewife.

Yet when women went to look for work outside the home, they faced a hostile culture. Friedan looked at psychology as it was shaped by influential voices such as that of Sigmund Freud, inventor of psychoanalysis. Therapists followed in Freud's footsteps when they diagnosed women who wanted jobs outside the home as driven by "penis envy"—that is, filled with a neurotic desire to have the power of men. Friedan, like de Beauvoir, wanted to combat the entire culture of women's inferiority and did so by taking on men's words about women and by analyzing women's own belief in those words. Although mostly writing about white, middle-class women, these two very intelligent pioneers laid some of the groundwork for further study of women's condition and the society that shaped it.

Another important body of writing that informed and continues to inform Women's Studies is the work of Karl Marx and Friedrich Engels, nineteenth-century philosophers and activists who built the foundations for a socialist analysis of women's situation. Their thinking argued that the oppression of women began with the institution of private property, which developed by overthrowing a system from the early days of human society in which land and tools were shared among everyone. The end of common possession of the earth's goods (from which comes the term "communism") and the subsequent creation of individual property led to the heavy regulation of women's sexuality so that there could be legitimate heirs to a father's property. Thus, the restraints on women and their inequality began. Marx and Engels had what is known as a "materialist" view of society and of history. In other words, the conditions of private property, production, and work under capitalism determined how society functioned. Once the material system of private ownership disappeared, there would be no more inequality among men and women. Instead, the return to a more communal or communist ownership by all people would provide liberation.

Marx and Engels's analysis influenced initial Women's Studies debates and often it still does in China, India, and Latin America. Scholars analyze the responsibility of global capitalism in which there are extremely wealthy owners of factories, financial institutions, and land for women's poverty, and they see the present-day flows of capital around the world as particularly oppressive to women. Other theorists used Marxist materialist concerns to dig into the conditions under which women lived and worked. In particular, they demanded that the conditions not just of work and production be considered important but the conditions of reproduction, including the birthing and raising of children. That the conditions of birthing and nurturing needed to be investigated as fundamental structures of life, just as work was, proved revolutionary in the university globally. Motherhood became a rich field for Women's Studies scholarship because of Marxist theorists and their new concerns.

Women's Studies grew up at a time of intense questioning of the social, political, and economic order, and many feminists looked to the communist countries for guidance. There was the thought that because all women worked in countries such as the Soviet Union (present-day Russia and the smaller satellite regions in Central Asia, such as Uzbekistan), East Germany, Hungary, China, and others, there was greater opportunity than in capitalist countries. Alongside the theories that made the conditions of reproduction important to study, the investigation of working women became a touchstone of Women's Studies. A concern to understand poor women's lives and their place in pre-capitalist and capitalist societies and under present-day global capitalism has also characterized Women's Studies research. Initially it was thought important to integrate women into Marxist theory in a more up-to-date way. Marx and Engels had described women's condition under capitalism a century earlier and women's situation had changed drastically since then. Women's strikes, their situation in the workforce, their political activism, and their poverty were thus crucial to an understanding of how to make society more just, and continue to be so. As some in Women's Studies saw the field's mission to study oppression, Marxist insights into the conditions of poor women came to underpin investigations that would become increasingly complex.

NATURE VERSUS CULTURE

A spinoff of de Beauvoir's question in Women's Studies has been about "nature" in all its forms. As women entered university in greater numbers, they did so in an atmosphere of general doubt. Women's nature, the belief went, was emotional and better suited to such nurturing activities as child care and home management than to the hard thinking involved in mastering university courses. Moreover, because women reproduced the human species, they were attached to childish things rather than to sophisticated reasoning. Women's Studies confronted and still confronts the prejudice about women's intellectual capacities.

There was a great deal of amateur writing that laid the groundwork for undermining the connection of women to nature. In 1970, the Canadian artist Shulamith Firestone published *The Dialectic of Sex*, in which she wrote that women needed to be liberated from their biology. Artificial wombs needed to be designed, so that women would not have to be hindered in their quest for jobs and lives of accomplishment. Far from being uplifting and "natural," Firestone claimed, childbirth was like "shitting a pumpkin." The attacks on women's nature and on their mutual relationship with nature continued in the press, while Women's Studies took up the issue by examining the conditions of women's natural lives or life cycles.

Anthropologists weighed in on the question of women's nature and looked more broadly at the extent to which women's lives and behavior were determined by their biology—or nature. The thought was that perhaps "culture" was the more important factor in shaping the course of women's lives. It was culture, they thought, that was the major force. In coming to this conclusion, examples from other societies proved decisive. Outside the West, for example, childbirth proved no deterrent to women leading highly active lives. Chinese peasants, the evidence taught, spent little time in childbirth and no time in getting back to work. Nature, it was believed, should take a back seat when it came to assessing women's capacities.

Instead the role of culture in shaping an image of women as more emotional and less rational than men, weaker and less capable than the "stronger" sex needed to be reexamined. Looking at school books for young children showed that early lessons in reading told highly gendered stories. The women in them were all mothers and wives, who tended the house and dealt with children. In contrast, the adult men left the home to work and provide for the family. They made the important decisions and took part in rugged outdoor activities. It was clear that men were the leaders and women the followers. School books as cultural products created the inequality of women simply through storytelling for children. Although the storybooks showed these roles as natural, Women's Studies judged them to be the result of culture. In fact, culture operated so that it made its own activities in creating hierarchical sex roles appear natural. In all sorts of ways, the superiority of men in societies was made to look as if nature had simply made men more talented and skilled than women, whom nature had made overly emotional.

The debate rages on. Women are often of slighter build and, according to scientists, have hormones that make them unstable before menstruation—that is to say, women are regularly and predictably unstable. Nature made women unreliable for leadership because they might have difficult decisions to make at "that time of the month." Having children and being responsible for their care would also weigh on women's capacity for focused participation in public life. Those wanting women's equality argued that all of this was cultural, not natural. Women have served at the highest reaches of government, and down to the present have been successful heads of state in the vast majority of important nations around the world except for the United States. It was culture alone that kept women in the home.

WOMEN'S STUDIES AROUND THE WORLD BROADENS THE QUESTIONING

Other questions emerged globally as companions to these, depending on specific national concerns, especially of post-colonial society. In India, for example, a government-sponsored study of women by researchers preceded and even sparked the university-wide investigations that began in the mid-1970s, and government funding and that of private donors fed research to help Women's Studies in India rapidly become one of the world's pioneers in the field. This initial report, "Toward Equality," helped guide the development of a parallel focus on poverty and literacy for women, some of the answers informed by Marxist analysis. Gradually and fitfully Women's Studies spread across Western Europe in the 1970s and 1980s. During this time women in Latin America were struggling against dictators, and with success in the 1980s, some of their early Women's Studies initiatives focused on political relations, especially those deriving from neo-imperialism alongside the more theoretical questions on the nature of women. Activists in Africa were also involved in national liberation movements during the formative years of Women's Studies in the West. They too responded to what they saw as the neo-imperialist programs for "development" from international organizations that were aimed at the continent: most of them affected women negatively by targeting men for development aid and by aiming to have active women marketers and farmers pulled out of the workforce and confined to housekeeping.

Health and motherhood along with women's economic well-being were at the forefront of questioning as Women's Studies programs developed in Africa in the 1980s and 1990s. We will examine the important questions arising in post-colonial nations in greater detail in many chapters but specifically in Chapter 4.

In yet another scenario, central and Eastern European teachers only felt themselves free enough to study women after the fall of the Soviet empire in the late 1980s and early 1990s. There had been many voices raised before then. In 1968, the short story "A Week Like Any Other" by Natalya Baranskaya appeared in the Soviet press and circulated like wildfire. It described a typical day in the life of an ordinary Russian woman scientist, including the stresses and strains of being a career woman, wife, and mother as most Soviet women were. The book resonated with the population at large. A Russian feminist, Tatiana Mamonova, published a collection of women's testimonials to their working lives under communism, sparking feminist debate. Mamonova cited specific accounts of discrimination and was sent into exile in 1980 because of it. Mamonova's crime was to document sexism in the Soviet system despite official assurances that the USSR was a workers' paradise. Women, as her anthology showed, were discriminated against, kept from important positions, and vastly overworked.

Once the Soviet system collapsed in 1989 and thereafter, many of these voices reappeared, some of them in Women's and Gender Studies programs. There were interactions with scholars around the world, thanks to financing by NGOs, but there was simultaneously a rejection of what came to be called "Western feminism." Women's Studies in the post-Soviet world led an insecure existence despite the efforts of researchers. On the one hand, the more open climate for academic research agenda motivated the kind of novel inquiry that the study of women offered. On the other, Women's Studies came to be seen as a luxury that a country in transition could not afford. Even more, it was also seen as an example of the kind of women's equality that had been a slogan of the old Soviet Union. Russians and those administering other post-Soviet nations wanted to escape the professed equality of communism to be more like the United States, where women's inequality was striking in terms of wages and lack of leadership positions. After increasing interest in the 1990s, Women's Studies declined in Russia especially with changes in the political climate and the rise of what one scholar has called the grand "automobile and harem culture" of the newly rich "oligarchs"—virtually all of them male.

CONCLUSION: ITS MEANING IS CHANGE

Women's Studies started the disciplines talking to one another around the investigation of women and sent researchers into archives or led them to consider data sets differently. It led others to reconsider what their methodologies were and what they should become in order to study women with non-sexist eyes. The result of Women's Studies in its early days was that new knowledge flooded into the world of education and that universities began to change. Women's Studies energized and motivated new groups of women, who themselves inspired snowballing new ways of thinking. However, there was great variety in programs and in the pace of development. Many women outside the West were gaining hands-on experience in national liberation struggles, nation-building, and anti-authoritarian activism that would shape Women's Studies in their societies.

In their postgraduate lives the many students from Women's Studies programs have entered every career path the contemporary world offers. Early on, Women's Studies graduates brought their skills to psychology, social work, and teaching. Others became lawyers, doctors, and politicians. Having sprung from feminism, some early graduates embraced activism, working for the relief of women's poverty, protection of the environment, and other women's causes. They were also committed to improving the overall situation of children and providing health care for underserved women and children. They also founded or participated in NGOs (non-governmental organizations) devoted to setting policies for political and social improvement or for skill and capacity building. In the long run, it has been the case that most Women's Studies graduates have been active in the promotion of democracy and equality in many different regions of the globe and often in worldwide organizations. This was just the beginning.

SUGGESTED READING

Arnfred, Signe et al. (eds.) (2004) *Gender Activism and Studies in Africa*. Dakar: Council for the Development of Social Science Research in Africa.
Boxer, Marilyn J. (1998) *When Women Ask Questions: Creating Women's Studies in America*. Baltimore, MD: Johns Hopkins University Press.

Sei-wha, Chung (ed.) (1986) *Challenges for Women: Women's Studies in Korea*. Shin Chang-hyun et al., trans. Seoul: Ewha Womans University Press.

Committee on Women's Studies in Asia (ed.) (1995) *Changing Lives: Life Stories of Asian Pioneers in Women's Studies*. New York: Feminist Press.

Du Plessis, Rosemary and Alice, Lynne (eds.) (1998) *Feminist Thought in Aotearoa/New Zealand: Differences and Connections*. New York: Oxford University Press.

Griffiths, Claire (2011) *Globalizing the Postcolony: Contesting Discourses of Gender and Development in Francophone Africa*. Lanham, MD: Lexington Books.

Jain, Devaki and Rajput, Pam (eds.) (2003) *Narratives from the Women's Studies Family: Recreating Narratives*. London: Sage.

John, Mary E. (ed.) (2008) *Women's Studies in India: A Reader*. New Delhi: Penguin Books.

Okuni, Akim and Ssewakiryanga, Richard (2003) *Post-Colonial Studies in Africa*. Kampala: Centre for Basic Research.

Ra-keum, Huh (2005) *The Nature of Women's Studies as Experienced in Feminist Research in Korea*. Seoul: Asian Center for Women's Studies.

van der Sanden, Jeannette (2003) *Truth or Dare?: Fififteen Years of Women's Studies at Utrecht University, 1988–2003*. Utrecht: Women's Studies, Utrecht University.

2

THE FOUNDATIONS OF
INTERDISCIPLINARITY

At first Women's Studies was a collection of subject matter from discrete disciplines, each contributing a literature, sociology, history, or psychology course from a scholar whose expertise came from outside Women's Studies. This was natural because scholars were trained to work in this way and students were only offered courses in traditional disciplines. Departments would free up these scholars to lend an individual course—say, one from sociology on women and sex roles or from economics on women in the economy—to make up a Women's Studies curriculum. Another course might look at famous women authors or famous women in politics or music. The possibilities were and remain endless for courses about women in religion, the arts, or philosophy. Researchers in Women's Studies followed the same pursuit of new knowledge for courses from within their individual disciplines out of a strong urge to expand the knowledge base of those fields. The idea for these researchers was that individual disciplines would soon come to incorporate the study of women, as a result of the massive rethinking. However, Women's Studies went far beyond that.

All these individual courses, such as women in history or women and science, still exist, but gradually there was experimentation: literature and history teachers offered team-taught courses, for example, while social scientists brought together information in a course combining knowledge of women in government, politics, and the economy, for instance. So, in the early days and even today, Women's Studies was and can be an array of courses about women coming from the individual disciplines in the university and more or less sandwiched together. A course in women and literature will come from the English or comparative literature departments with perhaps a psychologist or sociologist on board, while one on women and Buddhism will be offered by a scholar in the department of religion teaching with a historian. What happened in the early days of Women's Studies has often been called "multidisciplinarity" rather than true interdisciplinarity.

FROM MULTIDISCIPLINARITY TO INTERDISCIPLINARITY

The disciplines in Women's Studies could not help talking to one another, however, as students and teachers peeked over one another's shoulders to consider what the others were thinking and what their methodologies were. Historians learned from anthropologists and began using anthropological methods to write microhistories of women's rituals and everyday lives. Such microhistories looked at an individual woman, or at small villages where women led their lives in the context of family, religious, and other community structures— that is, in their cultural and social context. Topics such as sexuality, family, and conditions of work, reproduction, and creative expression brought the disciplines into more intense dialogue with one another. These topics often made the disciplines seem made for one another, as they clustered around a topic on women that brought interest from many points of expertise. One could look at the economics of the family, sex roles in the family, the literature and history of the family, and the family as represented in the arts and literature. Added to that were the sciences and the family: its genes, inherited diseases, and so on. Interdisciplinarity was being born in this amalgamation of perspectives.

It thus became increasingly common that clustered around the topic of women was the fusing of perspectives rather than their traditional separation. Courses based in disciplines continued to thrive and expand their audiences, but alongside those based in the disciplines were unique courses that fused intellectual perspectives and yielded courses best viewed in the round: women and aging was one example; women, culture, and society was another; women and sexuality, still another. There was instruction in "feminist perspectives on women" where the subject of women was looked at in a holistic rather than fragmented way. Such interdisciplinary courses are commonplace today, but some 30 years ago such a fusion made Women's Studies the leading academic interdisciplinary field, and from that intersection of disciplines came a broader move toward interdisciplinarity in the university as a whole. Cultural studies, ethnic studies, post-colonial studies, disability studies, and a variety of other interdisciplinary paths toward understanding emerged from the example of Women's Studies. This new field thus played a pioneering role in taking scholarly thought to higher levels of creativity and competence and in rethinking the way that knowledge might be pursued.

WOMEN'S STUDIES' EARLY CRITICAL EDGE

The question arises in many minds as to whether Women's Studies is an academic discipline, given its use of such an array of methods and insights. Women's Studies is additionally so new that it doesn't seem to fit in the traditional academic curriculum. So different is Women's Studies that for some critics who shudder at interdisciplinarity or don't understand it, the field is simply women getting together and complaining. This characterization sounds to those of us who have written many books and taught many classes to be the kind of slander aimed at undermining what is now a powerful intellectual field by those whose thinking has become outdated. Others maintain that Women's Studies can't be a discipline because it has no scientific or other method. It lacks standards such as those the arts have and has no "rigorous" methodology such as that the sciences follow. Because intellectual tools were shared and merged, the idea went, Women's Studies was simply a mish-mash, lacking scholarly weight or reliability.

Despite the critique, Women's Studies follows standard methods of inquiry. The first method to gain general acceptance was questioning the accepted truths and categories of particular disciplines. In history, for example, such questions abounded: "Did women have a Renaissance?" was one of the first, or "What would the Industrial

Revolution have been without women and why wasn't their presence acknowledged and studied?" In art history the question was "Where are the great women masters?" and "Why did art historians exclude women from their list of important painters?" We've already seen one of these questions in the nature versus culture debate. There was much rereading of the classics of philosophy, psychology, and the sciences from a Women's Studies perspective. For all their revolutionary nature, for example, French philosopher Jean-Jacques Rousseau's writings, from this perspective of re-evaluation, were seen to be traditional misogyny, redolent of theories of male superiority. Rousseau had to be viewed with fresh eyes because few political theorists took notice of his writings as a simple assignment of strict gender roles at a time in the eighteenth century when everything was open to question and reform. As a result of Women's Studies, Rousseau's political theories are now seen as an attack on the prominence women had seemed to gain in politics, literature, and society more generally in his time. Rousseau proposed their removal from public life and their confinement to the home, where they would raise the next generation of active, republican citizens. Not only Rousseau but many other thinkers who had never been scrutinized for their views on women were ripe for re-evaluation. Such revisionism is a standard tool of scholarship, not some expression of women scholars' wild emotions.

What followed was a critical look at the disciplines themselves—their values, their exclusions and inclusions, and their claims to provide universal truth—and this re-evaluation emerged to ground Women's Studies methodology. Women's Studies method can be said to involve a re-examination of old truths from a feminist or woman-oriented perspective as opposed to the male perspective on which disciplinary methods were traditionally based. Women's Studies scholars see this re-examination as based in objectivity, but objectivity used to eliminate or critique traditional scholars' male bias or misogyny. The idea was to evaluate male "truth" that was actually based on the exclusion of women, the devaluing of their achievements, and their erasure from important theories, analyses, and accounts of events. To the claim that previous standards were in fact neutral and "universal," Women's Studies scholars demonstrated male bias as at the foundation of truth-claims. From this vantage point, the entire composition of academic inquiry before feminism appeared to have been a celebration of women's absence from the canon of "great achievement" in all fields. In the sciences, it has even been shown that women are routinely omitted from scientific studies of the causes of heart disease and other important non-communicable diseases. Why is this so, Women's Studies asks, given the claims of scholarship as a whole to be fair-minded and concerned with knowledge over the entire field of human and natural experience? Thus, a series of questions about women's erasure has also shaped the field's methodology. Because these questions cross specific disciplines, they are at the heart of interdisciplinary method.

To correct these ideas, whether in sociology or literature, was to make women "visible." They had been erased and those erasures would not only be critiqued but investigated and undone. To make women visible was a tremendous undertaking and it continues to this day. Given the inattention to women's presence in the scholarly scrutiny of social structures, the construction of political models, or the development of scientific studies, there is the need for new statistics, formulations, projections, and general research that include women. The mimeographed booklet *Our Bodies, Ourselves* was published in 1970 by the Boston Women's Health Collective and made available precise information about the functioning of women's bodies. The work filled a massive lacuna in general knowledge about women's physiology and the conditions of their health. It also helped researchers and teachers understand the need for more teaching, researching, and theorizing of women's health in the academy, with the idea that somehow even biological knowledge about women was being withheld. Why was medicine so biased? Again, there was the recognition that when it came to health and the body, visibility was sorely lacking. To some extent this was so because of the carry-over of Victorian prudery and misinformation that was based on the premise that the population of women at large should be ignorant. Information about them was unimportant because they were unimportant. Again, the quest for information about women from a variety of perspectives helped create interdisciplinarity in which no individual discipline was primary; rather, the focus was initially on women.

For every new finding in a specific discipline, there was interest across the others in those findings. Researchers in the humanities, for example, were drawn to the information coming from such works as *Our Bodies, Ourselves* and were eager to use it. It was not long before historians were studying the power at work in women's relationships to doctors across the centuries or that others found themselves pursuing the history of midwives and childbirth. An anthropologist examined the treatment of women's bodies in medical textbooks, where in one instance from the 1980s, menstruation was described to medical students as the uterus crying out for a baby. She saw sexism in such metaphors—something that literary scholars alone might have done before there was interdisciplinarity and Women's Studies. Scholars in literature or the arts focused on the use of the female body in novels, poetry, and the great paintings done by men. Another breakthrough came with investigations of the way that the disabled body, for instance the pregnant body, was deployed to symbolize a disabled mind or spirit. It became clear that the female body had tremendous resonance but a resonance controlled by men and their interests. Such were the early insights that interdisciplinary methods—that is, the combined view from multiple disciplines—yielded.

The invisibility of women of color became an insistent concern that demanded methodological attention from all the disciplines involved in Women's Studies. In 1982 the work *All the Women Are White, All the Blacks Are Men, But Some of Us Are Brave* called for greater attention to black women and their erasure both from accounts of race and accounts within the growing field of Women's Studies in the West. Like others, Women's Studies scholars were called upon to discover facts hidden in archives about black women's lives. In this case as in others, there was inspiration from outside the academy, specifically from the black feminist movement. The Combahee River Collective statement (dated 1977) pointed to the invisibility and degradation of black women. That degradation, as black women scholars elaborated in their research findings, included the general disparagement of black women's intelligence in novels, journals, and political pronouncements. Simultaneously, interdisciplinarity shaped this questioning of the broader culture as well as the emerging field of Women's Studies. Representations of black women in scientific and political literature, in the history of empire and slavery, in health care and family life, and their raced work lives all needed attention. The idea was that Women's Studies methodology as used by white scholars was as blameworthy as male scholars had been in the erasure of black women from research concerns uniformly across the disciplines.

These are just a few instances of early interdisciplinary methodology and the issues that brought it into being. Findings crossed over discrete and separate academic disciplines to transform not only the study of women but the university itself. As Women's Studies evolved, it became clear that the ideas of visibility and of re-reading from new perspectives would resonate even more widely than in the early formulation of the field. Because many standard methods of analysis were used, blind spots about race and able-bodiedness—to name just two—were overlooked in the initial belief that the category "woman" was unitary and universal. It took a while for Women's Studies to expand its purview, address the complexities of and differences among women's lives, and broaden its analyses and methodological approaches.

Despite its shortcomings, interdisciplinarity advanced, though it took a while for everyone to appreciate its value and develop the breadth it called for. In fact, the interdisciplinarity that Women's Studies helped originate became a hallmark of contemporary, innovative academic pursuits. Today interdisciplinarity has spread to almost every major segment of the university from the sciences to the humanities and social sciences. There is hardly a discipline that does not interact with some other field—a far cry from the completely separate disciplines of the 1950s. Today, for example, scholars in English and languages engage extensively with the natural sciences, the visual arts, and psychology and psychoanalysis by learning their language, methods, and findings. Half a century earlier, majoring in literature had meant focusing on the literary work in and of itself— its use of language, meter, plot, and character. The sciences were also distinct and separate. Women Studies showed exactly how university research and thinking could break its own intellectual chains to become more innovative. It also helped the university as a whole consider how to take society on a more equal and just path by paying attention to blind spots such as race and to the gendered nature of claims to universal truth.

WOMEN'S STUDIES' NEW CRITIQUE OF REASON

Women's Studies increasingly depends on a major insight: that the scientific method and the subjects seen as valuable in the standard academic curriculum depend on masculinity and male values. If we take literature and history, for example, both of these disciplines have developed a canon centered on works by male authors and on the evaluation of these authors' genius. In history, describing the deeds of men, quoting them extensively, and being concerned with the inner emotions and thought processes of male leaders has been the discipline's subject matter. In contrast, the literary works of women are called "minor" and said not to have enduring value. Women "scribble" and men compose. Men are naturally brilliant, while women only work hard. Women's Studies investigates the formation of such literary standards and indeed all intellectual standards, finding that they simply reiterate social values—in particular, those stating that men are better than women and that white men are better than all people of color. Interdisciplinary investigation now shows how men and masculinity are taken as endlessly fascinating and worthy of ever deeper investigation in any and all disciplines. By contrast, women are not so interesting. In other words, Women's Studies methodology has given us the conclusion that beyond all the fancy rhetoric in literary criticism about universal standards of beauty, the vast majority of standards for assessing the worth of canonical literature are in one way or another affirmations of white male superiority and that the only way of affirming that superiority is to reiterate the contrast between superior men and inferior women.

The same reiteration of male superiority as the measure of value has been foundational for the disciplines as a whole, and uncovering it has been at the heart of interdisciplinarity in Women's Studies. The history profession developed around the idea that what happened in the West—that is, Europe and, increasingly, the United States—was the most important factor in the human past. Beyond that, the secret correspondences, public deeds, and wars waged by men were similarly more important than the private experiences of families or individual women. Again, Women's Studies helps show that so formulating the historical canon asserts over and over again that men's deeds are more important than those of women, and that this is the foundation of history's universal importance as it is in the sciences and every other field.

It is not just the subject matter that comes under scrutiny in evaluating the operation of the disciplines. Women's Studies opened a far more important critique in its early and ground-breaking exploration of the disciplines. Scientific methods, scientific values, and the scientific professions as a whole developed around male sociability and male control of professional practices. Even as they stressed observation and critical thinking, men formed scientific clubs, academies, and intellectual circles that considered male sociability as a crucial part of scientific investigation. In these groups, they shared their findings and groups would then discuss those findings among themselves. Seminars and scientific laboratories took shape in universities, and women were rigidly excluded from them. Doors of seminar rooms were even locked to keep women out. Men saw themselves as a group of equal "citizens" and part of a "republic" of like-minded investigators, unhampered by the family cares and small concerns of women. Thus, on the one hand, men were disinterested observers in search of unbiased truths, while on the other they upheld a rigid bias supporting a gendered, raced, and unequal intellectual order that saw women and people of color as inferior. Even after she had won two Nobel prizes for her work as a scientist, Marie Curie was excluded from the French Academy of Sciences because its members insisted that a woman could not have done such path-breaking work.

Early on, Women's Studies investigators showed that within the natural sciences most male researchers deployed a rhetoric about controlling nature, but nature seen as a woman. Ecofeminist philosopher Carolyn Merchant led the way along this path in *The Death of Nature: Women, Ecology, and the Scientific Revolution* (1980). Merchant is one of those interdisciplinary thinkers who pioneered Women's Studies because of her training in both science and philosophy and her engagement with feminism and women's scholarship. Her interdisciplinary analysis used the words of scientists such as Francis Bacon who helped create standards for modern science. For Bacon, the earth was a woman whose unpredictability, "insolence," and unpleasantness needed to be dominated instead of being allowed to romp about destructively. Practitioners of the new and rigorous scientific method needed to take control of this woman through their observations, the development of new knowledge, and the ensuing enactment of policies for nature's control. According to scientists, Merchant discovered, nature simultaneously was to be seen mechanistically as an entity that could be made to operate like a machine through correct analysis. Merchant's investigations also showed that science itself used the language of masculine domination as part of its procedures that would establish the new scientific disciplines.

The case was hardly different with the development of philosophy as a modern field. Philosophy evolved in the modern period to stress the importance of the "man of reason." This man of reason was pure mind, and his thoughts were likewise disembodied and removed from all the contingencies of the real world including physical needs. That is, the man of reason was not raced or gendered or sexed. When he used pure reason, he did so without a body, without emotions, and without such human characteristics as prejudice or religious enthusiasms. His perfection came from his release from all that was not mind. The man of reason thus stood in opposition to women, for example, who reproduced, menstruated, and concerned themselves with all the low tasks of keeping humans alive. Women dealt with food preparation, insect control, cleaning waste, disposing of excrement, and other nasty, earthy needs of the human condition—that is, women were condemned as inferior for filling the role in society to which society itself confined them. In creating this scenario, philosophy too was merely duplicating the values of male superiority and privilege and naming it "science." Who could possibly think that such clear-headedness was not superior to all the foul activities of women? Moreover, who did not know that women were not rational to begin with: had not playwrights and medical men, to name just two groups, shown women to be shrewish and hysterical—the opposite of the man of reason?

It was their inability to rise above the demands of ordinary life, the Western man of reason explained, that made women so poor at many of the arts and sciences. For instance, women could simply not transcend the smallness of their everyday lives to excel in mathematics or music. The abstract thinking required for math, for example, was beyond someone doing mindless household chores and mired in the routine of childcare and cooking. Women were also too sentimentally attached to children, small animals, and even their spouses to think grand thoughts. These preoccupations made their art, music, and literature banal and full of small-minded thinking. Women's thinking was clogged with false emotions or petty ones not the towering insights of men. Worse, it might be cluttered with descriptions of furniture, meals, and clothing.

In all of these examples, Women's Studies scholars, working across the disciplines, demonstrated that in fact the major scientists, critics, and researchers were unable to describe their virtues of their procedures or the define universal truths without invoking masculinity and femininity. That is, their methodology always relied on describing the inferiority of women themselves or of the realm of women, and these descriptions were foundational to men's explanations of what they did. There was hardly a field that did not follow this model in which anything having to do with reproduction or family life was degraded, while the work of men in the arts and sciences received approbation in comparison to female lives. Moreover, there were escalating attacks on women's emotional "shrillness" and their inability to work with others, usually evidenced by pointing out how "difficult" women artists and bosses were. All this stood in marked contrast to men's superior rationality. These were common findings of Women's Studies investigations based on using interdisciplinary tools.

Women's Studies scholars offered counterpunches of several sorts. Philosopher Diana Tietjen Meyers, for example, explained the functioning of the emotions—seen as feminine and thus inferior to masculine rationality—as in fact cognitive work. Emotions such as anger and fear developed from accurate assessments of situations and not from flights of fancy or women's instability. What was not mentally astute in an unarmed, isolated person's fear of a grizzly bear or a raging lion, feminist philosophers asked. Emotions, which women were said to have in abundance, actually served many purposes not only for the individual woman, who might have the wits to sense a dangerous situation such as a potential rape or other physical harm, but for the society as a whole. Fear and anger, to name just two emotions, could serve the cause of social justice in mobilizing activism to alleviate dangers to the wider population.

Women in the arts pointed to the outright masculinity that was celebrated even in arts said to convey abstract and neutral standards of beauty. Classical music was one of those so designated as a totally objective form. It was neutral, like mathematics, and moved according to rules and accepted patterns. Influenced by Women's Studies, however, scholars pointed to musical patterns said to be strong and "masculine" and others said to be weak and "feminine." These scholars mined the critical literature to show that even "absolute" music was gendered to reflect the hierarchies in society: masculine music deploying certain patterns indicated good music, while feminine music using other patterns was inferior. Likewise, some claimed that the female nude, the much-prized staple of male painting and sculpture, was less an expression of an artist's universal genius than of men's need for soft pornography in the days before photography.

Even though modern findings indicated that "the mind had no sex," in fact, people in the academy, politics, and society more generally believed that the mind *was* sexed and relied for justification of the male monopoly on cultural dominance on regularly talking about women's inferior minds. Philosophers had proposed the asexuality of the ability to think and reason, but at the same time male thinkers, distinguished in many different fields, worked hard to prove that in fact women's brains were in no way equal to the brains of men. By the eighteenth century, zoological illustrators had shrunk the size of women's craniums in their drawings and increased the size of their pelvic structure, indicating a dominance of reproductive power over mental power in women. In the middle of the nineteenth century, celebrated scientist Charles Darwin, whose influence only grew over time, determined that people of color and women were less evolved in their abilities than white men. Intelligence measurement in the form of IQ tests used questions about the type of carburetors in automobiles and about other male-centered activities to draw the conclusion that women were far less intelligent. Men seemed to be competing with one another to highlight women's alleged mental inferiority in what were supposedly scientific findings. The bottom line, however, was that Women's Studies had ferreted out the gendered flaw in definitions of reason and universal truth. Interdisciplinarity had made this possible.

ANDROGYNY

Amidst debates on nature versus culture and reason versus the emotions, the interdisciplinary question arose about whether alternative models of sex existed beyond the rigid stereotypes that seemed to exist worldwide. Had people thought in terms other than of male-female dualisms and restrictions? Across academic fields, the term "androgyny" was one early answer to this question, and it referred to a tradition in many parts of the world allowing for an individual to have both male and female characteristics. The history of androgyny went back to ancient times when certain deities encompassed many sex characteristics to signify power. Unlike the male god in the Judeo-Christian tradition, Greek beliefs envisioned, for example, Athena, who was goddess both of war and of crafts such as spinning. She and other gods and goddesses appeared in their images and in myths to embody behaviors that melded sex. Chinese thought valued the individual who could combine strength and compassion, rigidity and yielding. Celebrated women warriors of the past such as the Chinese maid Mulan and the French soldier Joan of Arc were similarly said to be androgynous.

Psychologists also suggested the existence of an androgyny of the psyche. Sigmund Freud, the Viennese founder of psychoanalysis, did much to break the sex binary when he wrote that most humans were born bisexual and that there was no clear path to adult sex roles. People could combine a range of behaviors and still lead satisfying lives. That said, Freud simultaneously explained that there were fairly standard routes to "normal" adult masculinity and femininity. In literature, writers had explored androgyny and gender fluidity. The novelist and essayist Virginia Woolf in the influential work *A Room of One's Own* announced that the creative person was generally androgynous in some way: "woman-manly or man-womanly." In the 1970s androgyny was a much explored topic across the Women's Studies curriculum through literature and the range of feminists who wrote about and even advocated androgynous behaviors and outlooks on life.

WOMEN'S STUDIES AND THE "L" WORD

Another alternative to the rigidity of thinking about men and women then at play in universities and in society more broadly was considering sexual orientation and sexuality from an interdisciplinary perspective. The activism of lesbians pushed scholarship to consider the erasure of lesbians not only from history generally but from the budding attention to sexuality in the social sciences, sciences, and humanities. Once again, the first scholarship involved overcoming the invisibility that lesbians suffered both in research and in society as a whole. The first studies to appear recovered lesbian literature or explored the sociology of lesbians as a group and within groups.

Women's friendships and Boston marriages were other subjects that initiated the field. At the beginning these studies focused on white women, but Chicana and black lesbians raised their voices about the more thorough lack of attention both to them and their achievements. Finally, in the early days of Women's Studies some lesbian authors demanded attention be paid to the heteronormative condition of scholarship as a whole—not just as a field. Rationality and research were not only sexed as male, they were heterosexed as straight. These lines of thinking developed interdisciplinarity further, forming a unifying insight that would shape and even revolutionize methodology in ever richer ways in the future.

Lesbianism advanced Women's Studies methodology but it was also used to attack the field. Despite the low esteem accorded to Women's Studies by some administrators and faculty members, the popularity of Women's Studies remained steady and it failed to disappear as some hoped. One way of combating this popularity and women's attraction to this course of study has been, and remains, to call women taking and teaching in Women's Studies "lesbians." If heterosexual women were held in lower esteem than men, then lesbians were seen as lower than heterosexual women. Some debated this point, suggesting that lesbians were sexually and personally less threatening to men and thus more acceptable in the workplace than straight women, whose presence challenged standard categories of women's place. Whatever the case, there came to be the association—and one that would last down to the present—of Women's Studies and anyone associated with Women's Studies with lesbianism. Even today, most students in Women's Studies programs mention that they are regularly accused of being lesbians by their fellow students when it is discovered that they are enrolled in a course about women or gender. Additionally, family members will express worry that their children are becoming queer in these courses.

The heteronormativity—that is, the holding up of heterosexuality as a norm—characteristic of academic thinking and of society as a whole was thus confirmed. Students today share strategies for dealing with such accusations and worries. Some say "yes, we are all lesbians, all ten thousand of us," which can stop the conversation cold. Others use the opportunity to open conversations with family and those students willing to discuss sexual orientation and hetero-normativity. They explain what Women's Studies is and how it can help in getting jobs, building esteem, or providing skills that can make the future more humane and sustainable. Above all, they affirm lesbians as valued members of the Women's Studies community and as its leading thinkers. The importance of both investigating and challenging heteronormativity would become increasingly apparent as scholarship moved towards deeper levels of thinking about sexuality. Making sexuality visible formed another foundation for future interdisciplinary development.

MARGINS AND CENTERS

As Women's Studies was developing its interdisciplinary metho-dology, male scholars still saw everything they did as the center of scholarly advance. Indeed, the word "central" was used often in scholarship to describe the main issues or the pivotal cause of events, and these usually involved men. There were central ques-tions about politics and society as well as a sense that there was a central cause to an event, trend, or political consensus. Historians and literary scholars talked about those figures who were the center of social progress or whose work was at the center of debate. Until Women's Studies came along, those who chose the core or central issues were male scholars who were themselves at the center of the university. Those people at the center of scholarly concern as actors were also men, both from the past or in the present.

Women's Studies researchers acknowledged as a thought experi-ment that male deeds were at the center of important investigations of politics, economics, and society. They addressed the question of "centrality" in several ways. The first was to interrogate the criteria for naming something as central. Were all the male writers who filled anthologies to the exclusion of women really "central" to the literary canon? Were not excluded objects of study such as families and households just as central to an understanding of society as class and other categories that were said to be central to social structure? Sexuality, race, sex discrimination, and a host of other topics were argued to be at the core of society and thus in dire need of inves-tigation to achieve a more accurate scholarly picture of the whole and its "centers."

A second tactic, and one that has become pivotal in Women's Studies, has been to explore life from the perspective of those who have been pushed to the margins of society. The homeless, impoverished, family life, criminality (especially of women), and those who draw or write from a position on the margins of society are important for what they reflect about the society as a whole. Those on the margins are also the vast majority of people and thus as important to understand as those very few at the center. In fact, many people who might belong at the center have been marginalized simply for being women. One thinks of inventors who could not hold patents in their own names because they were women. The result was that their husbands received the credit for many an important development, making the center seem more pivotal than it actually is. The center might in these cases be said to be illusory so that examining the margins helps one find both ordinary and extraordinary actors—many of them women. The center existed because creative activity and superiority were automatically assigned to men or because law codes constructed male centrality.

When it came to women, most of them were at the margins whatever their status, race, or religion. The exploration of the margins began. *Women at the Margins* is the name of an influential book by the renowned historian Natalie Zemon Davis. In it, Davis presents the lives of three women of early modern Europe who have heretofore been seen as marginal and who indeed operated outside the power centers of their day. Marie de l'Incarnation was a Ursuline nun who left her family and went to North America. There she worked with Native Americans and constructed a major dictionary of Native American/French language. Maria Sibylla Merian, a scientific illustrator, traveled to Surinam and other regions beyond the Netherlands to draw plants. Davis points out that from the margins, Merian drew differently, showing plants in their various states of development and illustrating the insects living from those plants. Finally the Jewish housewife and merchant Glikl bas Judah Leib had her share of trials, as did other women at the margins, but she pursued an active life to ensure family well-being despite the problems her children posed to that well-being. In Davis's account, the margins are places worth studying for they are full of activity, special trials, and enduring accomplishment. Another foundation had been laid.

MAD WOMEN IN THE ATTIC

At the margins of the margins were those women who initially made activists, scholars, and ordinary people nervous. Women's Studies began drawing into its orbit characters who were initially seen as "mad women," a characterization often applied to women as a whole. As the feminist movement burst onto the scene, activists and women scholars were often seen as a bit crazy and ordinary women, it was said, were prone to a variety of mental disorders. Tranquilizers were administered to women in large doses to treat the many feelings of helplessness, the aches and pains, and the nervousness said to be normal in women—in contrast to the rational behavior said to be normal in men. Women were confined and lobotomized, when they were not treated with kid gloves to keep their everyday insanity in check.

Women's Studies took a hard look at the so-called "Madwoman in the Attic"—a term alluding to nineteenth-century author Charlotte Bronte's novel *Jane Eyre*. Bronte's heroine, Jane Eyre, is a governess for the dark hero Mr. Edward Rochester. During the course of the novel strange occurrences—violent and even vampire-like ones—occur in Rochester's mansion. Ultimately it comes out that Rochester's wife, whom he had married most unwillingly because of her madness, had done these bizarre deeds and that she is responsible for burning down the mansion itself, blinding and maiming Rochester in the process. The presence of this madwoman in fiction eventually sparked the creativity of Susan Gubar and Sandra Gilbert, two professors of English, to compose *The Madwoman in the Attic: The Nineteenth-Century Woman Writer and the Literary Imagination* (1979).

Gubar and Gilbert pointed to the themes of confinement and madness, of darkness and witchcraft, and of exclusion that dominated women's fiction. Emily Dickinson, who lived in relative isolation in Amherst, Massachusetts, was one of their examples, as they picked out her assertive allusions even as she herself was defined as timid and withdrawn. In pointing to the complexities of Dickinson's life and art, they reminded readers of the "double bind" of the woman at the margins, in the attic, or relegated to the home—even the nursery. Gothic writing, they claimed, captured that ambivalence in featuring mansions and other places of confinement but a confinement that was so bizarre and exaggerated that it fulfilled the need for assertion. Moreover, Dickinson finds the day an oppressive male time period, preferring, like the seventeenth-century Sor Juana de la Cruz, the night as the time for female assertion. In sum, like the madwoman in Bronte's story, reversals of value and bizarre female assertions are strategies for women's literary voice. They lead to an understanding of life at the margins from an interdisciplinary perspective that has characterized Women's Studies. With further research the margins too would become populated with a greater diversity of women, including the impoverished, raced, differently oriented sexually, and those with non-normative bodies.

CONCLUSION

It was rarely smooth sailing with Women's Studies. Beginning in the 1980s critics from an array of countries mounted an attack against it and other fields that were coming to gain a place in the academic curriculum. A focus on the artistic and literary works of women, it was said, was replacing the great classics in painting, literature, and music. African-American novelist Toni Morrison, for example, was taking the place of Shakespeare, while British sculptor Barbara Hepworth was sacrilegiously being exhibited alongside such greats as Henry Moore. In Europe and the United States, even the insertion of writers who created the extraordinary Latin "boom" in literature was seen as dragging the culture down. Attention paid to women's issues in newly emerging countries was said to drain energy from the overall well-being of the new nation. Women's Studies, it was said, was another version of Western imperialism. Wherever it sprouted, there was a justification for squashing Women's Studies.

It was no accident that the "culture wars" against women's and minority scholarship in the West took place alongside the rise of Pacific and Latin American economies. Japan, Taiwan, South Korea, and others in the Pacific as well as Brazil and Chile in Latin America experienced soaring technological growth, while the West's share of the global economy steadily declined. The American mind was "closing", in the words of one critic, as the works of women and minorities undermined "excellence" in the name of multi-cultural representation. There was no room for democracy when it came to judging the quality of literature, art, and work in math and the sciences. Achievement in these fields had always been the purview of white men, as pseudo-scholars such as Charles Murray appeared to demonstrate. To Murray and others, with their supposedly "objective" assessment of the world's leading intellectuals, human accomplishment mainly arose in societies with a dominant European ethnicity and with male leadership.

Such were the grounds for attacking Women's Studies and the battles were often heated. Nonetheless, as these first two chapters have shown, the foundations had been laid from the late 1960s to the early 1980s. Questions of nature versus culture, issues of race, sexuality, class, illiteracy, and able-bodiedness, and a focus on the supposedly gender-neutral basis of the "scientific method" had all been addressed in preliminary ways. These foundations laid, Women's Studies would now deepen its probing of gender, race, poverty, sexuality, violence against women, and the new globalism of capital. As it became an established academic field, its intellectual terrain would gain a more definitive shape, but a no less stimulating one.

SUGGESTED READING

Conway-Turner, Kate et al. (eds.) (1995) *Women's Studies in Transition: The Pursuit of Interdisciplinarity*. Newark, NJ: University of Delaware Press.

Zemon Davis, Natalie (1995) *Women on the Margins: Three Seventeenth Century Lives*. Cambridge, MA: Harvard University Press.

Gubar, Susan and Gilbert, Sandra (2000) *The Madwoman in the Attic: The Nineteenth-Century Woman Writer and the Literary Imagination*. 2nd ed. New Haven, CT: Yale University Press.

Hawkesworth, Mary E. (2006) *Feminist Inquiry: From Political Conviction to Methodological Innovation*. New Brunswick: Rutgers University Press.

Krook, Mona Lena and Mackay, Fiona (eds.) (2011) *Gender, Politics and Institutions: Towards a Feminist Institutionalism*. New York: Palgrave Macmillan.

Luxton, Meg and Mossman, Mary Jane (eds.) (2012) *Reconsidering Knowledge: Feminism and the Academy*. Winnipeg, MB: Fernwood Pub.

Minnich, Elizabeth Kamarck (2005) *Transforming Knowledge*. 2nd ed. Philadelphia, PA: Temple University Press.

Moran, Joe (2010) *Interdisciplinarity*. New York: Routledge.

O'Barr, Jean (1989) *Women and a New Academy: Gender and Cultural Contexts*. Madison, WI: University of Wisconsin Press.

Westbrook, Lynn (1999) *Interdisciplinary Information Seeking in Women's Studies*. London: McFarland.

3

INTERSECTIONALITY
AND DIFFERENCE
RACE, CLASS, AND GENDER

Women's Studies began with other unifying themes, and one of them was the common idea that women share an identity as women. In the early days of second wave feminism the idea was that anywhere one found a woman, one found a sister. Women shared the same life stories of oppression; they all operated on the margins; they symbolized madness in opposition to men's rationality; they were, as Simone de Beauvoir put it, a collective and individual "Other." There is thus in many writings about women the idea that they are essentially alike, whether because they are intellectually inferior, automatically frivolous or nurturing, or often nobler than men because of a shared womanly virtue. At the beginning of the women's movement and indeed one of the common denominators of the women's movement is the idea that they together have some special quality that unites them all as women. As one Indian feminist said in the 1930s, women "were all sisters under the sari" (Chaudhuri 2004: 130).

Belief in the commonality and lack of individuality of women was also an idea shared by the culture as a whole and promoted by male writers over the centuries. That women were all the same in their inferiority was and remains a widely held belief. They simply lacked the rich individuality and wide-ranging capacities of men. The women's movement, it is now seen, merely reversed the evaluation, making it positive. Feminists pointed to women's sameness as worthy mothers of citizens, their unity in being oppressed, and their innate value and even virtue. Women were all sisters, and they were all good. Soon after the founding of the most recent women's movement, however, the idea of "difference" as opposed to an essential unity or sameness offered a challenge. Indeed, studies have made the idea of difference a pivotal idea in Women's Studies. But what is difference and how does difference operate? The feminist theorist Donna Haraway gives one evalutation: "Some differences are playful; some are poles of world historical systems of domination. Epistemology is about knowing the difference" (Haraway 1990: 223). Often difference can be the foundation for domination—let's say of women by men, of blacks by whites, of local peoples by colonizers, of the physically weak by the strong, of the rich by the poor, and so on. Others have come to see a recognition of difference as key to building coalitions across various interest groups. This chapter sorts out the many forms of difference as they have shaped Women's Studies.

Scholars, feminists, and activists began dissenting from the initial belief in the innate similarities that made up a single "womanhood." Did lesbians have the same interests as straight women? Were rich and working-class women really sisters? In the classroom, were students supposed to feel a commonality with their teachers? It was asked whether the Maori of New Zealand shared a bond with women of European descent, given the oppression of local people. Thus many came to see that differences of all kinds should be emphasizing the importance of women as subject matter. Differences among all women, past and present, in varying parts of the world, in all walks of life, of varying races, ethnicities, and social status needed to be highlighted. The unity once attributed to women as a sex and gender is now repeatedly contested. Difference creates the rich and the poor, the gay and the straight, the raced and the unraced. The issue of difference is one that provokes questioning and that has led to some of the most important innovations not only in thinking about women but in thinking about society, the economy, and politics more generally.

Many Women's Studies thinkers and activists in newly independent countries have little tolerance for the concept of difference, a major protest coming from women in India. They believe that the focus on difference gives frivolous attention to "identity," "personality," and other cultural issues when in fact there are large political and economic structures governing and oppressing the lives of women and men alike that need analysis. Paying attention to shades of difference is a luxury women in emerging countries needing solidarity with men can't afford. We consider this critique at greater length to show both that considering difference raises controversy and that it has also changed Women's Studies and the way many disciplines think about their subject matter. Like interdisciplinarity, the concept of difference has provided a totally new perspective from which to study human experience. It is now at the heart of much Women's Studies thinking, including the thinking of its critics.

CONTESTS OVER DIFFERENCE

In the last chapter we mentioned the voices raised across the West by African-American women and lesbians in the women's movement, who pointed to the lack of representation of their concerns in the social and political activism of the 1960s and 1970s. The Combahee River Collective made evident the special differences between black and white women and between black women and black men while also raising issues of different sexualities. The Collective criticized the dominance of white women's needs in the women's movement and the blind eye turned to women of color among civil rights activists. The authors of *All the Women Are White, All the Blacks Are Men, But Some of Us Are Brave* made many of the same points, focusing on a range of differences among women in the past and present societies and in university life itself. A distortion in scholarship and teaching, these critics of Women's Studies maintained, occurred because of the invisibility of black women both in the civil rights movement and in Women's Studies and women's politics. Cherrie Moraga in *This Bridge Called My Back*, pointed to the differences among women of various ethnic and racial groups and of non-heterosexual sexualities, and like the Combahee River Collective, charges white lesbians with excluding the concerns of women of color, especially ignoring Chicana lesbians.

These examples from the United States were not exceptional. In Australia, the descendants of indigenous peoples pointed to the same exclusions and homogenization in Women's Studies and the women's movement. Women's unity and sameness simply did not exist, they claimed, and the first peoples of the continent had a different past and present from the white settlers. Migrant women into the West from former colonies such as Buchi Emecheta also announced their "second-class citizenship," while Native Americans in the western hemisphere similarly denounced their ongoing invisibility and oppression by whites, including white women. The eruption of difference as pivotal to Women's Studies worked a transformation in the way scholarship and classroom life unfolded. More importantly, the interdisciplinary study of diversity and difference made Women's Studies more of a pioneer than ever in broadly reshaping intellectual inquiry.

The articulation of difference was an explosive issue and early on was seen as a threat to the coherence of Women's Studies as a discipline. The argument went that Women's Studies was so threatened by conservative forces in the university and in society at large that differences need to be overlooked. Instead, common goals and practices need to be emphasized. Differences can be seen to be small, whereas the good of the whole—whether it be the women's movement or Women's Studies or even the well-being of the world's women—needs to be the prime concern among teachers and scholars alike. Unity, not difference, is primary, some activists claimed, even as they criticized the universal thinking among men for hiding systems of domination.

Other challenges from the emphasis on difference have arisen, notably in the struggle to discern whose differences are weightiest and which groups face and have faced the greatest discrimination. Were the most oppressed those women whose ancestors had been slaves and who continued to suffer from racism? Is it the women of Afghanistan, as the Western press has announced for the past decade, whose oppression should be seen as primary or even that of all Muslim women? Women in cultures where genital cutting is a tradition are also seen as those whose different treatment relegates them to the top rung on the ladder of oppression. Pundits came to call these articulations the "oppression Olympics." Because the list of oppressions is in actuality a long one, for some time there has been confrontation, especially when monetary assistance to underserved groups is at stake. Just as important, the listing of differences can tend to make those in the wealthy countries of the North feel superior, especially as they agitate on behalf of those whose differences weigh them down. Those in wealthy countries where benefits are many can see those who dress differently, worship differently, have different diseases, and suffer a different level of poverty as pathetic and backward.

The debate over difference and the drive to overcome it raises once again the debate of nature versus culture and revives older paradigms. For some, there remains a common core that eradicates differences: that is, biological cycles and reproduction govern women's lives, to some extent, in a way that they do not for men. Essentially, women are women and the differences raised as problems by those of different sexualities, races, and ethnic groups may be said to be superficial in comparison with the oppression of women generally. This general oppression spreads across all these racial divides and across class differences. The commonality of women's situation and of their experienced lives is greater than all differences.

A somewhat related but common criticism of difference comes from women in once-colonized countries where the idea of differences separating male and female and women from one another is repugnant. United with men in colonial oppression and in opposition to it, women have a solidarity with men in the struggle to make their independent nations thrive—just as they acted together with men to obtain freedom in the first place. In fact, for many in these nations, their biggest differences are with Western women, especially Western feminists. One South African activist pointed to the lack of interest in a Western-style equal rights struggle with South African men. "To argue that African women should concentrate on and form an isolated feminist movement ... implies African women must fight so that they can be equally oppressed with African men" (Smith 2000: 69).

Finally, the idea that there were differences among women including many different points of view and needs challenged the mainstream scientific principle that there were universal laws and truths. From the Scientific Revolution of the early modern period and the eighteenth-century Enlightenment, there was a growing sense that no matter what an individual's religion, status, gender, or personal biases, one needed to overcome such differences to attain universal truth. One's nationality or ethnicity, for example, should not prejudice one in favor of one's nation when judging policies and analyzing facts to draw conclusions about international politics.

Although we have seen the problems with the gendering of reason that scholarship in Women's Studies probed, there remains a belief that truth can be discovered—despite the claims of difference. We will see theories in Women's Studies challenging that unity too.

While Western people in Women's Studies fractured these universals into differences, many outside the West fought to uphold universal rights and the rule of law as greatly needed. These supporters held that laws should apply to all people regardless of differences and that rights guaranteed by law are for everyone. Initially the idea of universal rights enforced by a national government was meant to overcome the centuries-old practice of local nobility or landowners, for example, dispensing judgments and punishments while being themselves immune from any overarching codes of law and rights. Under slavery, the enslaved African had far fewer rights in the New World than did whites and until fairly recently women lacked the right to their own wages, and to custody of their children in case of divorce. So eliminating all differences when it comes to the application of law has been a progressive cause and one advocated by the feminist movement. Nonetheless, some see "human rights" and the push for "democracy" as simply another "civilizing mission" of the West, one used to justify military invasions. Still, women in academe, whether students or teachers, wanted to be judged by universal standards instead of giving men special privileges. Higher grades or higher salaries—that is, salary or grade differences simply because someone was male—needed to give way to a universal standard applied without reference to gender difference. Yet even this idea was contested when it went against local traditions or when it seemed to be dictated by the West.

At the same time, the concept of difference helped pull Women's Studies into tighter interdisciplinary cooperation. The concept of difference allowed Women's Studies to examine issues of race, class, and gender from an integrated set of perspectives and thus fostered interdisciplinarity's progress. Exploring the various aspects of difference led to the concept of "intersectionality"—a term that has become increasingly central to Women's Studies methodology. Before the development of this term, scholars often argued about whether race, class, religion, ethnicity, or gender was more important. The concept of intersectionality proposed that these aspects of difference intersected and needed to be considered in tandem with one another. Eventually intersectionality expanded in usefulness. For example, it helped explain the interplay of feminism and nationalism in independence movements and the intersection of religion with other categories of identity.

RACE AND THE BIRTH OF INTERSECTIONALITY

Race is currently a powerful marker of individuals in politics, the economy, and society and one that brings out expressions of difference. Today race is often used as a visible way to categorize people as different, and even the governments of many countries make citizens indicate their race on census and other forms. People in ancient times in Europe had a myth that the different races were simply baked for different amounts of time, with whites having been baked for the least amount of time and blacks for the longest period. Other shades of skin color came from cooking for intermediate lengths of time. Interestingly, this early articulation of race combined equality and difference in less harmful ways than today.

In our modern age, geneticists find only the tiniest difference among so-called races, but this has not prevented entire societies from calculating worth on skin color and labeling skin color and other physical signs as indicating "race" and inescapable difference. Once race is produced as a category it converts into a murderous form of difference that in the past determined whether one was a slave or free, which is not to say that slavery was necessarily based on racial distinctions. Africans simply took as slaves those they captured in warfare. Afghans raided across Russian borders to get anyone they could capture and sell for a profit into slavery. In other words, the association of race with slavery has never been a consistent one.

Nonetheless, over the past five hundred years, since the beginning of modern slavery and colonialism, race became a powerful weapon used to justify oppression. Although slavery has unfortunately existed among humans for millennia, we see that the beginnings of modern empire by Europeans produced a powerful ideology of race. In that ideology, blacks, Native Americans, and eventually Asians were seen as inferior and thus only worthy of manual labor. This ideology only developed fully over time, because at the outset of European world travels most travelers marveled at the advanced civilizations outside the West. In fact, in the sixteenth century as colonialism took hold,

Europeans were skilled at virtually nothing except making guns and orienting themselves on the sea. Otherwise, as one economist has put it, their standard of living was no better than that of Neolithic humans down to 1800. Other "races" were vastly superior.

For women slaves from Africa and among Native Americans, the development of racism was disastrous, despite women slaves in the New World being full of agricultural knowledge compared to the white men who owned them. Nonetheless, non-white women's bodies were said to be animal-like and monstrous. Those justifying slavery additionally declared women of color coarse rather than delicate and sexually loose and lewd. They were meant to be worked hard, raped, and made to bear children. In South Africa, for example, the rape of a "colored" woman or girl might go completely unpunished, while a man of color who even looked at white woman could well be prosecuted. In the post-slavery United States that same man would be lynched and his body mutilated.

Because of this special history, the existence of a common racial experience among the descendants of slaves in North America launched "black feminism." For some, as we saw in the Combahee Collective's manifesto, this commonality was in the blood, making the statement suspicious to some as almost duplicating racial arguments traditionally used to create categories of inferiority. For other thinkers, black feminism was a perspective on black women's experience of abuse and racialization. This perspective or "standpoint" consisted not only of experience but the process of working through the experience of discrimination on the basis of race and gender. It also held within its standpoint the legacy of black women's enslavement and the vast variety of black women's conditions as they produced knowledge.

What became even clearer during the development of a global women's movement, however, was the lack of similarity among women of color. Black women from North America could be and were seen as privileged in our contemporary world compared to those in more southerly parts of the globe. Women of color were accorded different kinds of treatment and places in the social hierarchy based on the degree of color in their skin, and men could actually choose them for their skin color. Ethnic solidarity and identity could also profoundly affect the standpoint from which women of color operated and the situations they had to work through. Thus global location and local values shaped and separated women of color alongside race, gender, and class distinctions. Religion, too, could come into play, making intersectionality an extremely complex tool for analysis.

The awareness of race has become enriched with the use of "critical theory," a way of thinking that aims to uncover social problems and oppressive use of power. Offshoots of critical theory include critical race theory and critical legal studies, which examines the ways in which supposedly neutral laws are in fact representative of a white male position on society and justice. Critical race theory looks at the ways in which laws actually discriminate against everyone who is a minority. So, beginning with critical theory, we arrive at a point of having critical race feminism—a race feminism that allows for the critique of laws and social values from the point of their intersectionality.

Intersectionality is an idea initially devised by Kimberlé Crenshaw, a professor of law in the United States. She explains how the concept of intersectionality was born. As an undergraduate at Cornell University, she found no courses that covered race and gender at the same time, even though in her own case and in that of many others, race and gender were intertwined, burning issues. They were burning issues for very practical reasons that become apparent in the situation of black women before the law. For them, dealing with injustices was like a car wreck. "If you're standing in the way of multiple forms of exclusion," Crenshaw explains, "you are likely to get hit by both. First the race ambulance medics come and say, 'sorry, you need the gender ambulance'; they are followed by the gender ambulance whose medics tell them to call the race ambulance." The law, she found, had no way of dealing with wrongs done to women of color because judges had trouble figuring out whether the harm was a racial harm or a gender harm. In these cases, they tended to throw up their hands (Thomas 2004). The problem is that the law (or society more generally) doesn't recognize the interaction of exclusionary positions and identities. That interaction she calls intersectionality.

Intersectionality is at work in everyday life. In the United States, white men could and did justify their exclusive hold on power by explaining that they were needed to protect white women from the lusts of black men, bringing race and gender together. Moreover, the woman of color is said to be dangerous to civilization because of her particular combination of black and female animality, as was implied of Anita Hill in the confirmation hearings of an African-American Supreme Court justice. The hearings showed the attacks of white male senators on a black woman law professor, suggesting both her lesser rationality and her excessive sexuality ("a little bit nutty and a little bit slutty," one senator called her) in order to defend a black male candidate for the high court. The intersection of race with class and gender occurs across the western hemisphere and around the world, escalating with global migration. As West African and other Muslim women move to Europe, their religion, race, class, and gender all come into play in what is most often outright discrimination on multiple fronts. Their jobs are worse, their customs and daily practices suspect, and access to their sexuality is regarded as a right. To make their bodies visible, they may not wear their traditional enveloping clothing. Thus these exclusions come together in particular ways that will be different still for women of other constellations of identities. A recognition of inter-sectionality allows for the crafting of unique solutions to the variety of intersecting conditions.

ETHNICITY AND INTERSECTIONALITY

Many Africans maintain that ethnicity is a far more powerful marker among African peoples and that race has far less to do with the conditions of life than do such differences. There has been genocide among the Hutu and the Tutsi ethnicities as a legacy of colonialism, for example. Alongside this one African example, eth-nicity resonates in other parts of the world, with a real and some-times fatal impact on women, who are singled out for both their sex and ethnicity. In the European Balkans, which have long experienced so much of a mixture among peoples that it is difficult to tell one ethnic group from another, the production of an impu-ted "ethnicity" as something essential to identity has similarly led to genocide and "ethnic cleansing"—that is, attempts by one group to totally eradicate another through mass murder and starvation. There has also been ethnic cleansing of Armenians by Turks and by Germans of Slavs and Roma. Distinct groups, whether genetically different or not, have been said to constitute separate ethnicities.

The Botswana-born feminist author Bessie Head wrote movingly about ethnicity, race, and gender in her novel *Maru* (1971). The heroine of the story is from the much despised "Bushman" ethnic group in Africa, but she was given shelter and an education by a white missionary so that she came to be "refined" and an able teacher. Once she moved to her teaching post, the intersection of ethnic, racial, and gender identities came into play in her life. She was an undesirable—despite having valuable "white" skills—for being of a lower ethnic group. Additionally, the heroine's life is shaped as powerful men take an interest in and make use of her on the basis of gender and ethnicity. In this novel intersectionality is at work as a mixture of race, ethnicity, and gender determined the outcome of the story and the fate of its characters.

In contrast to the slow unfolding of intersectionality in this fictional account are the persistent and horrific instances where men rape women of different ethnicities (and religions) as a way of defeating the men they see as competitors or enemies. This has happened around the world, with the most notable recent instances in civil wars in Congo, Sudan, and Bosnia. In such instances the idea was to ensure a triumph of an ethnic group either by impregnating women so that the child would bear a competing ethnicity or by so dishonoring women through rape that male honor would be damaged. Such intersections of ethnicity and gender, as with the intersections of race and gender under slavery in the western hemisphere, have left huge scars. Nonetheless, because rape is often accepted as a "normal" condition of women's lives, until recently rape under these conditions has not aroused much concern. Intersectionality has added to the understanding of such atrocities, even opening onto the subject of the participation of other women from opposing ethnicities in perpetrating them.

CLASS AND INTERSECTIONALITY

Another major category of difference is class, which has been defined variously as how much money one has or how one lives one's life in terms of consumer and other choices—a "lifestyle" definition of class. There are also definitions of class that have to do with status and power relations, such as might be found in families with an aristocratic past or simply in families that have long held the reins of power in a city, region, or even entire nation. Women around the world have recently been elected to high office—in the Philippines, India, Indonesia, and elsewhere—because of their family connections and as members of the elite or upper class.

A Marxist definition of class, which influenced many early feminist scholars, talks about class as based on relationships to the means of production. The way in which goods are produced by humans leads to class distinctions. In slave society, for example, there were those masters who owned slaves and possessed the land on which they worked and those slaves who were propertyless and completely under the control of the master. In modern industrial or capitalist society, there are those (Marx called them the bourgeoisie) who owned all the means of production. They owned private property in the form of factories, mines, and modern transportation or large tracts of land on which grain and other major products were grown to sell on the market. They controlled high finance and the mechanisms of regional, inter-regional, or global trade. Everyone else worked for these people and thus comprised the working class. Propertyless workers could vary in their wealth and status, from being day laborers to being expert scientists doing research for large companies. Workers could own houses in which they lived or automobiles, but this was not the same as property that produced goods and wealth—the private property that Marx and others have criticized down to the present.

In liberal ideas of equal opportunity, the classes balanced themselves out and might come to live harmoniously. For example, the shopkeeper and her worker were a sort of couple in which the worker sold his labor to the shopkeeper and in exchange the shopkeeper paid him. It was a balanced relationship in which work was exchanged for pay. Moreover the idea among liberals that everyone had equal opportunity at birth led to the belief that anyone could become a shopkeeper or a multi-millionaire business person. For Marx and Marxists, the bourgeoisie and the worker can never be friends because the owner of a factory is always out to make money for his or herself and will do so by paying the worker as little as possible.

In fact, for Marx and for the communists who came to power in Russia, China, Cuba, and North Korea, their movements triumphed when working people came to recognize that the roots of their oppression lay in class. They took action: Marx founded international working-class organizations. With direction from leaders like Vladimir Lenin, Mao Zedong, and Fidel Castro, workers fought to overthrow their governments, whose laws and police force upheld the domination of the capitalists. There was no need in their minds to do anything special about women because they interpreted capitalism and its system of private property as at the root of women's oppression. In fact, they scorned feminists as "bourgeois" and middle-class; that is, not concerned with the problems of working people.

Women's Studies scholars take class seriously, though they blend various definitions of class and have many opinions about what class means. One common concern is the impact of capitalism on women's lives. Their concerns are that women under capitalism are always victims of the profit motive by which they are most exploited. Men are always valued more than women as workers in terms of pay. This means that there is a gendered wage gap based on the idea that men simply get more money than women. As historians have shown, the same roughly 70 percent wage gap has existed at least since the Middle Ages, when working women earned 70 percent of what men did for the same work. In other words, they see what Marx did not really see—that gender and class work together in ways that need study and understanding in order to right wrongs. Women's Studies sees that only by understanding intersectionality can there be a true understanding of women and class.

Class intersects with gender and with many other forms of identity in constructing social reality. In terms of class and gender, one sees that there is already cause for dissension among men and women, since women are statistically disadvantaged in the economy. Intersectionality is at play in this analysis and class and gender have operated in tandem with one another—let's say in the job market. At the same time class and gender have operated with religion, ethnicity, and race not only in the job market but in politics and cultural life. Western employers in parts of the Ottoman Empire and former Ottoman Empire used religion along with class and other markers of identity to structure the job market hierarchically. As it affects women in global women's activism, class has operated to privilege certain voices—initially those of middle- and upper-class women who helped organize the women's section of the United Nations or those who assumed leadership positions in the international conferences sponsored by the UN. Using their own expressions of intersectionality, the voices of those indigenous, lower-caste, abused religious and repressed ethnicities have combined to question the privileges assumed by those of higher class and whiter races.

PLURALISM AND ITS CRITICS

Once difference and intersectionality have been acknowledged, pluralism becomes, for some, a remedy for the problems that difference can bring. Pluralism maintains that all kinds of difference can co-exist in some kind of peace, if not full-blown harmony, or that they can bring tensions to the fore in fruitful ways. For politics, a commitment to pluralism fosters the coming together of people from possibly competing groups to form alliances capable of bringing about change, enacting a policy, or preventing public harm. Pluralism can operate even around issues on which different groups might disagree when they all decide that it is better to work together and forge a compromise position. The development of "rainbow coalitions"—that is, alliances of people of many philosophical, religious, racial, and political hues—now happens regularly among feminists and other groups to make action possible even where difference is pronounced. An acceptance of pluralism is often seen as crucial to Women's Studies classrooms.

Nonetheless, even pluralism takes work to achieve useful outcomes among those with differences. Often unacknowledged differences have wreaked havoc among would-be allies. There are those among feminist thinkers who dismiss the idea of pluralism as unproductive. The argument is that pluralism is too ready to accept difference without really thinking about what differences mean. Pluralism is Pollyanna, reeking of the idea that we should all simply get along, regardless of the inequalities among groups. In contrast, recognizing differences among women forces us to reflect on the meaning of difference itself as a general concept. Differences also allow us to be critical in new ways, some of which we will examine below. Nonetheless, the advocates of pluralism as a strategy in today's mass society think that it is the best solution for women, given the complexity of the gendered world in which we live. Black men and women may not have the leisure to discuss the finer points of gender difference in a racist world; solidarity is their goal. There are times of crisis when women of the global South and the global North have allied to devise plans of action, as at Beijing in 1995.

EQUALITY VERSUS DIFFERENCE

The concept of difference poses many other problems. Is the main difference one among men and women, as many people seem to think, including those in the early second wave feminist movement? The question of difference when it comes to men and women is especially fraught given the feminist movement's drive for equality, but also given its simultaneous drive for consideration of women's differences. For example, feminists strive for equal pay and equal job opportunities. At the same time, they want women to have maternity leave and access to good health care both for themselves and their families. The Swedish system of state support for motherhood, as it was devised in the 1930s and spread to other European countries, provided such benefits. Swedish women have access to jobs and simultaneously good pay. In many other countries this has not been the case. The need for maternity leave or for time off for childbirth itself makes employers reluctant to hire women because of their high-cost needs based on their sexual difference. How can women demand such costly benefits, the argument goes, and such different treatment and still claim to want equal treatment in the workplace? Men receive no such benefits. Why, on the basis of equality, should women?

After World War II, as feminism was struggling elsewhere, Sweden and other Scandinavian countries forged ahead on the course they had begun earlier. Not only did they give women maternity leave, they gave families parental leave and even came to legislate that men take some of that leave time to participate more fully in parenting. In the United States, by contrast, these issues came to a head in the Sears case of 1984–85 in which the Equal Employment Opportunities Commission brought a suit against the retailing giant Sears for failing to let women serve as sales people in high-commission positions. The evidence mustered by social historian Rosalind Rosenberg showed that women preferred lower-pressure jobs so that they could devote time to family and household responsibilities. By contrast, labor expert Alice Kessler-Harris claimed the opposite was true in her findings: throughout history, women had sought better jobs, mostly to support themselves and their children. Union women took equal pay and access to good jobs as the motivation for all their organizing efforts. There was no woman who did not want equality of opportunity and pay in the workplace.

Others saw difference as a rallying cry for feminists throughout history. Karen Offen, a US scholar of feminism in Europe, noted the presence of "difference feminists" in the nineteenth and early twentieth centuries. This type of feminist did not want rights for women on the basis of equality but on the basis of the difference and complementarity. Indeed the phenomenon was also spotted in US feminism, where activists in the past believed that women's differences from men—especially the fact that they gave birth to children—gave them special qualities that men did not possess. On the basis of this difference, women needed to participate in the public sphere to balance out the qualities men possess. These male traits included ambition, rationality, and aggressiveness—to name a few. They needed to be balanced in the making of public policy by the feminine characteristics stemming from motherhood. Feminine qualities were empathy, nurturing, pacifism, and other good things. Public policy would benefit greatly from an equal measure of these differences in the political world. Thus women should have the vote and hold high office to bring these differences into a harmonious balance.

Activists from the post-Soviet world have more recently emphasized women's differences. Tired of being overworked, underpaid, and generally abused in the name of equality under communism, these activists also stressed women's special needs. They needed to be appreciated and allowed to beautify themselves in ways denied over the decades. There had been little room for romance and love in the Spartan conditions of the Soviet empire because of the emphasis on comradeship and struggle to make communism a reality first in the face of civil war, then during World War II, and finally under Cold War conditions. Whereas feminists in Western Europe and the United States might need more equality and want to get work in the public sphere equal to men's, women in the former Soviet sphere needed acknowledgment of their femininity—that is, their difference—after their exploitation under communism. They wanted to be "loved" and pointed out that Western feminists who emphasized equality had no idea of what equality meant in practice.

These activists also doubted that feminism as articulated by women in the United States and Western Europe had any relevance to their lives because of insurmountable East–West differences.

When the Sears case was resolved against the women who had wanted equal opportunity, it was a shock to many. The court judged that women actually did not want better conditions because they had other priorities than work. Working women were indeed different from working men, the decision claimed, to the extent that getting ahead was less of a priority for them than having a stable family life and caring for children. For women, economic achievement came second to quality of life because women were different. Equality was not their first priority and this prioritization of family life explained their failure to reach high positions. Sex discrimination had nothing to do with the monopoly of men in high positions in Sears.

The situation seems impossible to resolve, and in fact, as we will explore in detail later, has been analyzed as part of an irreconcilable binary or pair of oppositions. These binaries are impossible to resolve because they work together as one another's opposite without which the other would not exist. In the case of equality versus difference, there would be no equality or concept of equality if difference did not exist at the other end of the spectrum. Would equality have any meaning as a term or in practice if there were not difference to which it could point as undesirable? Without difference, would not equality be meaningless and not even exist as a concept? Thus, as a pair, it is hard to disentangle equality and difference even though jurists, feminists, government officials, and others have clearly tried to do so. Struggles for equality and difference go hand in hand and are actually inseparable.

CONCLUSION

As we have suggested, the priority given to the study of difference and intersectionality has not met with uniform approval. One main criticism is that Women's Studies and women involved in activism need to focus on points of solidarity in order to devise pathways to change. This includes the solidarity of men and women, middle- and lower-class activists, straight and queer, and people of different races. In fact, one critic claims that oppressive institutions in the global economy and national politics have perfected the art of segmenting groups according to difference. One sees in the workforce that it is segmented into lower and higher pay grades not because of skill but because of race, gender, or religion. Similarly, political platforms segment groups into minorities to be disparaged as a way of getting votes: in the United States in the 1980s, the group was "welfare queens", defined as African-American women. The virtues of solidarity have been seen in women and men joining together in anti-colonial movements or in those for social change and civil rights.

The importance of understanding difference and intersectionality, however, seems just as pronounced. Recognition of difference and intersectionality breaks the pattern of women as all being the same and having a common "essence" that defines them. Such recognition also allows for the creation of more functional alliances among groups after differences and common interests have been struggled with and sorted out. Understanding difference and intersectionality can be said to produce more realistic appraisals of the individual, group, and more general human behavior and additionally lead to more informed discussions of equality, freedom, and power. Without an understanding of difference, the power of dominant groups is masked by a commonality of interests that is often false.

SUGGESTED READING

Berger, Michele Tracy and Guidroz, Kathleen (eds.) (2009) *The Intersectional Approach: Transforming the Academy through Race, Class, and Gender*. Chapel Hill, NC: University of North Carolina Press.

Chaudhuri, Maitrayee (ed.) (2004) *Feminism in India*. New Delhi: Kali for Women.

Crenshaw, Kimberlé (ed.) (1995) *Critical Race Theory: The Key Writings That Formed the Movement*. New York: Norton.

Thornton Dill, Bonnie and Zambrana, Ruth (2009) *Emerging Intersections: Race, Class, and Gender in Theory, Policy, and Practice*. New Brunswick: Rutgers University Press.

Haraway, Donna (1990) *Primate Visions: Gender, Race, and Nature in the World of Modern Science*. New York: Routledge.

Jónasdóttir, Anna G., Bryson, Valerie and Jones, Kathleen B. (eds.) (2011) *Sexuality, Gender, and Power: Intersectional and Transnational Perspectives*. London: Routledge.

Lutz, Helma, Herrera Vivar, Maria Theresa and Supik, Linda (eds.) (2011) *Framing Intersectionality: Debates on a Multi-faceted Concept in Gender Studies*. Farnham: Ashgate.

Lykke, Nina (2010) *Feminist Studies: A Guide to Intersectional Theory, Methodology and Writing*. New York: Routledge.

Smith, Bonnie G. (ed.) (2000) *Global Feminisms Since 1945*. London: Routledge.

Taylor, Yvette, Hines, Sally and Casey, Mark E. (eds.) (2011) *Theorizing Intersectionality and Sexuality*. New York: Palgrave Macmillan.

Thomas, Sheila (2004) *Intersectionality: The Double Bind of Race and Gender*, Perspectives: American Bar Association. Online. Available HTTP: <http://www.americanbar.org/content/dam/aba/publishing/perspectives_magazine/women_perspectives_Spring2004CrenshawPSP.authcheckdam.pdf> (accessed 16 June 2012)

Wiegman, Robyn (2012) *Object Lessons*. Durham: Duke University Press.

4

GLOBAL AGENDAS

Women's Studies programs have flourished across the globe for decades. Initially these programs focused on women in individual national cultures—their economic situation, health needs, family and social life, political status, and cultural achievements. As our world has changed, Women's Studies increasingly considers the state of women in our interconnected world. Even as Women's Studies developed new categories of analysis, it became evident that dramatic transformations were bringing economic interconnections and the rapid communication of knowledge. One thing that these revealed was the vast array of differences among women depending on where they lived in the world. The experiences of women were shaped by global differences and shared commonalities as never before. These connections—often unequal, at other times shared—have become central issues in Women's Studies.

Women's Studies looks at the global forces that shape the lives of women. Multinational companies—that is, companies that have a workforce and operations outside a national base—continue to increase in number and scope, for example. They globalize the workforce by moving operations to whatever location can offer the cheapest labor. Often this labor is female, sometimes operating in countries with corrupt or dictatorial regimes and subject to the conditions of free trade, including a lack of protection for workers. In this chapter we explain such concepts and powerful structures as multinationalism in industry, free trade regimes, the World Bank and the International Monetary Fund—all of which have advanced the interconnections in the world economy that have affected women, usually unequally. We also look at the global conditions causing women's migration and their oppression in civil wars and famines, using these to explain the Women's Studies term "location," the connections with Peace Studies, and the gendering of human rights. The contested relationship between North and South is also examined in light of Women's Studies insights and of the critiques of local and global activists.

The interests of women from wealthy Northern societies, many argue, have too often determined both Women's Studies' and feminist concerns. Thinkers in the global South first pointed to this dominance, or at least influence, as they developed the field of Post-colonial Studies. Post-colonial Studies has brought to the fore questions of the subalternity of women, most notably those in the global South but in fact everywhere that patriarchy, especially white patriarchy, rules. This chapter explains women's "subalternity"— that is, their lower status—in the context of colonialism and global capitalism. There is also the sense that around the world Women's Studies serves as a symbol of a kind of modernity that also arose from Western power. In this critique, white women's lives and ideas are taken as a model for "modern", that is, desirable institutions and thoughts. We will look at the idea of modernity and its relationship to women and the rise of Women's Studies, along with its spread globally. In fact, even the category "woman" was in some cultures created to show progress where it had not existed before. These lines of thinking and the sharp criticisms of the West and Western feminism will be explained.

Finally, we ask whether globalization has brought the world's women closer together at all and if so, on what terms. There have been high-profile international conferences dominated not by women from the global North but by women from the global South—showing their superiority in terms of organizing and concern for a wider range of women's issues. The evidence suggests that satellite communications, the internet, air transportation, and the globalization of culture have allowed women to see and communicate with each other, sometimes bringing greater empathy and also bringing differences and disagreements out in the open. The research and activism of women from the global South have been pivotal to expanding Women's Studies' accomplishments.

THE LEGACY OF EMPIRE AND POST-COLONIALISM

The ending of colonialism and the rise of new, independent nations replacing colonized regions are major background elements of today's globalism and its impact on women's lives. Between 1945 and the 1990s fully independent nations emerged from the control of imperial powers such as Britain, France, the Netherlands, Belgium, Japan, and the United States. Additionally, the countries of Eastern Europe and Central Asia freed themselves from control of the Soviet empire in 1989 and thereafter. The process involved the activism of men and women alike, especially at the grassroots where women were important activists. In movements such as the Mau Mau against the British Empire in Kenya, the Algerian war for liberation from France, or the Vietnamese struggle for independence from Western domination generally, women operated supply networks, acted as messengers, planted bombs, and served as soldiers. These struggles built women's political and military skills, while making use of their organizational, economic, and domestic aptitudes.

In some cases, when colonized peoples freed themselves from imperial and colonial structures, the process entailed a military struggle. Men in the emerging new nations took up arms, occasionally with women fighting alongside them but more often serving as crucial support networks providing medical care, information, and food. Liberation by force of arms led to military dictatorships in many of the new nations, often because both US and Soviet governments during the Cold War from 1945 to 1989 were eager to supply increasingly plentiful and sophisticated weaponry. The high value placed on military institutions determined who would be in power, and in many places military prowess had given men positions in the colonial armies. Even before that, many Africans and Asians had been skilled warriors serving their individual kings, chiefs, and other local leaders. Then, during the Cold War, the United States and the Soviet Union competed to provide weapons, airplanes, and tanks to leaders of the newly independent countries in order to win their loyalty and business. The resulting militarization and escalating sale of arms globally has meant continuing violence against and the massive rape of women long after states had thrown off colonial rule. Genocide has occurred in some areas because under colonialism the imperial powers had pitted ethnic groups against one another as part of their divide and rule strategy. Imperialism and the arming of the world's peoples with increasingly powerful weaponry have left a legacy of violence in women's lives down to the present, as women in many regions continue desperately to search for physical security, sometimes by migrating to foreign lands.

The enduring legacy of colonialism shaped the advance of Women's Studies outside the West. India, African nations, and several in South America immediately began addressing issues such as poverty, lack of education, and violence against women left over from colonization and decolonization. Whereas the colonizing powers often educated local men so that they could serve as agents of imperial rule, women received virtually no education. Some nationalist leaders since the early twentieth century had stated that the goal for their new nations would be to educate men and women equally and to bring women out of their "backwardness." In many areas, independence leaders specifically wanted women to be more modern—that is, more like women in the West—and to improve their condition.

Government researchers in India began Women's Studies in this atmosphere of both concern for women's elusive well-being and determination to study the causes and devise solutions to their poverty and the regular violence inflicted on them. When doing so, the fact that Europe, the United States, and Japan had dominated or tried to dominate Asian and African regions from the eighteenth century to the 1950s was seen as a major cause of women's difficult situation. Elsewhere, from the sixteenth to the nineteenth century, Spain and Portugal had ruled South America and a portion of the Caribbean as slave economies, while the United States and Great Britain exercised economic and political power indirectly over the region. Even as Britain lost its empire, it maintained a financial hold on many places, while the United States expanded its grip via powerful business interests and military intervention or the threat of it—practices called "business imperialism." The grip was in large part economic, motivated by a determination to keep profits flowing out of the country or to those at the top of the political ladder. The result was foreign and domestic exploitative poverty for many ordinary people, especially women. Thus, outside the West, Women's Studies began from what is now called a post-colonial perspective. It challenges Women's Studies students in Europe and the United States to look beyond issues mostly affecting white women or those local women who, along with their families, have benefited from colonialism or business imperialism.

THE POST-COLONIAL PERSPECTIVE

A post-colonial perspective in Women's Studies means examining relationships among the peoples of those countries that gained independence after World War II and the nations from which they became free—that is, examining imperialism's long-lasting consequences. Not only have Women's Studies scholars looked at the relationships between the colonizer and the colonized, they continue to determine what those relationships became after colonization. So the aftermath of imperialism is as important as imperialism itself. There is also an interest in women's activism both before and after colonization in both nationalist and feminist movements. One major question is: What were the effects on women who lived under colonialism and their legacy in relationships into the present? The answers have been incredibly complex, given the fact that imperial, colonial, and other relationships with the West lasted in many cases for several centuries and that the effect on women was pronounced and remains so.

Imperialism means the domination of the people of one country by another, creating an empire where economic and social profit gained by any means is primary to the foreign rulers. Colonialism occurs when communities of settlers arrive from the dominant country and work to set up the region as a working colony, upsetting the normal patterns of life for local people. In the early days of Western imperialism, colonialism and imperialism had a range of consequences. Before there was actual domination, Europeans had depended for their success on women traders and their commercial experience, networks of influence, and information about trading. In India, women of influential princely and other families tried to arrange marriages with English men in order to tie British merchants into the Indian system and thus profit from the European presence. Other women became the concubines, intermediaries, and language teachers of foreign men—"dictionaries," as these women were called. Increasingly European and later Japanese and American men brought particular hardship to women, as imperialism and colonialism led to new kinds of economic arrangements, especially the privileging of local men in occupations that were once women's such as agriculture and landholding. Europeans also put local men in charge of districts where once women had had a voice in community decision-making. Imperialists often harassed or actually attacked women sexually. The multifaceted oppression worked its way into culture.

Modern imperialism brought unprecedented brutality in the twentieth century and armies of conquest and occupation meant sexual enslavement for many women. When Japan occupied much of East and Southeast Asia during World War II, the army rounded up women, especially Korean women, to serve as forced sex workers. When the Allies defeated the Japanese in 1945, many of the brothels were simply turned over to the US army for its use. Germans in World War II, as part of their own imperialist expansion across Europe, set up brothels in concentration camps. Women prisoners were granted special favors such as more food and better housing in return for having sex with male prisoners who had "earned" the right to sex because of their hard work or exemplary behavior. If one of these women became pregnant, she might be shot or, alternatively, released—the reasoning behind these erratic results is still unclear to observers. The legacy of imperialism and imperial wars remains important to an understanding of women's position in the global economy and in the global social order.

WOMEN IN THE GLOBAL ECONOMY, PAST AND PRESENT

Women have long worked in an economy that was global. The prime example is the slave woman, whether an African seized in warfare and sold to Europeans to be transported to the western hemisphere or one taken and sold in the lucrative Saharan or Red Sea trade. Russian women were abducted by Central Asians and then sold across the continent. For millennia, women have been held in varying conditions and made to do domestic, sexual, or agricultural labor. Today there exist women migrating globally—voluntarily or involuntarily—to engage in all these forms of labor either because of opportunity or because of outright coercion. Additionally women from at least the sixteenth century down to the present have engaged in agricultural labor for others, producing rice, cotton, cocoa, tea, and other products to be marketed around the world. Many labored on plantations set up by owners from the imperial powers or in the processing of sugar, tobacco, jute, and other products. Increasingly, their work lives depended on the expansion of capitalism to affect global markets in products such as palm oil, and this meant that large-scale merchants from the most powerful business institutions could set the terms of sale.

Although women in non-Western countries had built their lives around work in agriculture and textile production, often for global markets, by the second half of the twentieth century the development of the multinational corporation affected their opportunities for work more directly. A multinational corporation is one that has expanded from its home country to set up branches of its businesses around the world. Nestlé, the Swiss food manufacturer, is an example of a multinational corporation dating from early in the twentieth century. From the 1960s onwards multinational corporations were numerous, with the United States initially having the largest number. After 1990 multinational corporations were headquartered in Brazil, Mexico, Britain, Japan, and the United States—to name just five points of origin—but ran plants, did banking, hired a workforce, and organized marketing in many places outside their home base.

Multinational corporations moved their operations to wherever labor was cheapest—their sole interest in the people of any locality or nation. They often had guarantees from dictators of an ample supply of cheap female labor. Moreover, authoritarian governments promised that these women would be hard-working and not complain about long working hours, minimal wages, and unsafe conditions. Should these women workers protest in any way or exact a higher wage, the multinational corporation would simply move its operations to where another pool of labor, often com-posed of women migrating from outmoded farms to the city, would accept the low wages and bad conditions. Thus, women were to be docile and excessively hard workers even as they often brought the largest supply of foreign currency into their home country through this labor. This was said to be their contribution to nation-building; that is, women's overwork in factories was a patriotic duty.

WOMEN AND NEO-LIBERALISM

The term "neo-liberalism" is often applied to the economic system increasingly in place during recent years. This term is an economic and policy one in which governments favor businesses by not regulating them and by not taxing them. The term means a "new liberalism," harking back to the eighteenth and nineteenth century before there were any rules to protect labor, any insurance programs such as social security and accident insurance, or any taxation on businesses. These centuries were the heyday of liberalism, which basically meant "laissez-fare" or do as you want. Neo-liberalism opposes the benefits of the welfare state where children are educated in public schools, where families have health care, or where adults have accident insurance and other benefits at work. This is old-fashioned liberalism from the nineteenth century by which each person is on his or her own against corporations and where there is no government protection for individuals—only for businesses. Multinational corporations from the 1980s on worked hard to restore economic conditions by which workers would have no benefits or rights and where unions were banned. The main goal in neo-liberalism is profit; any direct contribution by corporations to human well-being—including paying a living wage—reduces profit and is thus something the believer in neo-liberalism would stamp out.

Women globally have from time to time protested the grip of multinational corporations on their lives and on government policy. Multinational corporations are cozy with dictators around the world, especially for the way authoritarian regimes herded unprotected, undemanding workers into their factories. In South Korea in the 1970s women rose up against conditions in electronics factories—the harassment and sexual assaults along with inhuman working hours—and were beaten by government soldiers. Their protests were so determined and the brutality inflicted on them so vicious, however, that eventually they helped bring down the South Korean dictatorship. In other areas, women organized to educate and organize themselves to alleviate the worst conditions of neo-liberalism—the favelas (shanty towns) outside Rio de Janeiro were one location for grassroots activism as we shall see later. The control of countries via their economies thus relies on women's correct behavior in foreign factories. It is not only women who have been menaced, of course;

recently male workers in foreign factories in China have committed suicide over the bad conditions.

Woven through these stories of abuse are more positive ones, showing that human experience even of neo-imperialism is complex. In China, rural families choose which single daughters to send to work in European toy factories or Taiwanese textile plants located in China. These young women perform repetitive, demanding work with long hours that sometimes last more than a day without rest. Yet they learn to move from plant to plant to gain small advantages either in pay or conditions in the few years during which their families send them to make money in the city. People learned new skills: "The first time I saw those English letters I was scared to death. I couldn't recognize them, so I copied them down and recited them at night," one young Chinese worker recalled of learning English (Ngai 2005: 83). With the influx of manufacturing jobs, educational standards rose, along with access to birth control and other medical care that improved health.

WOMEN'S MIGRATION IN A GLOBAL AGE

Women predominate as the world's global migrants and their numbers have soared in the past 15 years. Right after World War II, women from the Caribbean moved to Europe to work in the new hospitals and other institutions of the growing welfare state. Often young women are sent by their relatives, as we saw in the case of China, from the countryside to the city to work in factories. Filipina women, both skilled and unskilled, travel to virtually every continent of the world to serve as domestics, service workers, nurses, and occasionally as professionals. Today, women from Sub-Saharan Africa migrate, legally or illegally, to Europe, which in the nineteenth century was the region with the greatest out-migration. Once in Europe they usually begin in the lowest jobs no matter what their education. There are exceptions to this downward mobility: in Paris in the 1990s a Congolese woman named Thérèse set up small restaurants, serving Congolese dishes, playing Congolese music, and selling Congolese products. She was an illegal immigrant who benefited from her relatives' work for international airlines, which allowed her to import African goods easily and cheaply. Worried about the police and often changing her location in Paris, she nonetheless prospered.

Women thus come from poor countries, mostly moving to find opportunity and to ensure their survival as well as that of the families. Many of them, like Thérèse, think of themselves as mobile subjects, even permanently on the move. Several Jamaican women, interviewed in the 1990s, regularly migrated with friends and relatives from Jamaica to Canada, Great Britain, or the United States. It was a way of life, but with Jamaica and networks there was always a base for the care of children and the maintenance of family relations. The vast majority of these mobile subjects serve in what has come to be called "care" work and form expansive diasporas, traveling to places where they have connections or know of opportunities. Entire families, often mobilized by women, can be on the move to various parts of the world to support the family core in the nation of origin. Even if they have the same skills, they may suffer different fates in terms of finances and status within the society. For example, a Filipina woman going to Rome will most likely end up as a domestic worker, whereas the same woman going to Los Angeles may find more varied opportunities and experience differences in terms of acceptance and rejection. Diasporas can themselves have varied expectations for those who join them in terms of national identity, sexual conduct, and group loyalty. In short, the quest for economic security for the family has many components beyond the economic one, and Women's Studies focuses on understanding this complexity.

Especially in times of economic crisis, the migrant can face varying degrees of hostility and discrimination. She is, in the face of racial and class hostility, virtually defenseless because she is outside her nation, working for strangers of a foreign nationality, and obeying a foreign set of laws. Besides being denationalized, she generally does not have her family to give her support and strength in the face of racism and the threat of violence. Instead she operates in the context of globalization's large structures, which directly affect her well-being and from which she gets little protection from her own nation-state. It is this situation that, in part, rouses some non-Western activists to see Western feminist concerns about sexual identity, for example, as frivolous.

Nonetheless, migrants' situation, according to some, should be categorized as "transnational" rather than as global to the extent that the home nation-state often arranges with another for work visas for migrants. The nation-state does so because the funds that return to the home country add to the nation's well-being and sometimes constitute a third of overall income. Because of this income stream, there may be both compulsion to migrate and some kind of protection even abroad. Yet Women's Studies questions that protection because many transnational migrants are secreted over borders for vast sums of money and kept imprisoned as workers until they have paid off that debt. Even after paying it, one Thai woman reported that her entire barracks of workers was told that they still owed money. They were only assisted by their home country when the United States government discovered their situation and released them. Other countries ban or limit women's migration in the hope of boosting population or keeping women's unpaid labor at home. As we will see in the last chapter of this book, the situation of world migrants combined with new conditions of sexuality and evolving Women's Studies theories has produced some startling and innovative ideas about our human condition more generally.

WOMEN AND POVERTY

In many Women's Studies programs around the world the issue of women's poverty was uppermost from the outset. Although it was sometimes seen as a sort of subset of class, there are many who see poverty as a special condition apart from traditional ideas of class. Poverty became an issue of its own for some thinkers and policy-makers, needing analysis and solutions beyond any definition of class. According to the United Nations, "Women perform 66 percent of the world's work, produce 50 percent of the food, but earn 10 percent of the income and own 1 percent of the property." Additionally, women comprise 70 percent of the world's poor, and their poverty may be found in every country, including those of the wealthier countries of the north. In this regard, poverty and womanhood may be said to belong together, with poverty seeming to inhere in some essential way to women.

During the UN-sponsored Beijing Conference on women in 1995, delegates focused on issues of women's and girls' poverty, including their lack of access to clean drinking water, adequate food, medical care, shelter, and safe living conditions. What might be called core feminist values that shaped the movement from the beginning—political and civil rights, for example—gave way at

Beijing to the urgent concern for women's poverty. Although representatives at this global conference called for women's free participation in elections and in national leadership, it became evident that women from the global South wanted attention directed to the impoverishment of women and the dangerous conditions in which they lived out their lives. The necessities of life were missing in the lives of perhaps a billion women around the world.

Women from the North were perhaps shamed into acknowledging their own wealth, and there was even a degree of astonishment, as the contentious side of women's poverty became apparent. At the Beijing Conference, African-American participant Malika Dutt recounted her expectation that women from nations of the global South would be less experienced and capable because of the less developed economies they came from. Thus, it was not apparent to all delegates that women's poverty was the main issue. Moreover, even women of color like Dutt felt animosity directed toward them from African and Asian women from poorer countries. US and other women of color from the global North faced hostility because of their comparative wealth, not a sense of ethnic or racial community these more privileged women had expected (Smith 2000: 305–13).

Poor women, however, have become fetishized by by some of the most powerful global institutions, including the World Bank and a range of NGOs. These institutions made poor women emblematic of the condition of the "Third World" countries, post-colonial states, or emerging economies as a whole. As Chandra Mohanty signaled more than 20 years ago, this depiction of the impoverished woman as pathetic makes Westerners, including Women's Studies scholars, feel superior because their wealth and education so greatly surpass that of such a woman. How is the subject produced and regulated and how do businesses profit from the focus on women's poverty? (Roy 2003: 22)

DEVELOPMENT AND WOMEN'S POVERTY

Poverty, especially that of women, has been made into big business, feminist scholars and other investigators maintain. For one thing, poverty has been "feminized" in officials' minds, with the argument that women are the subjects of abuse and discrimination at the hands of unreliable men. As a result the largest and most powerful organizations such as the World Bank have focused a great deal of public attention on women's poverty—more in fact than on almost any other social problem. Since the demise of outright occupation of regions by the colonial powers, there has been a big push for economic "development" in the newly emerging nations of the world, with one of its stated aims being to bring women out of poverty. Women's poverty becomes the rationale for intervention by global institutions, foreign nations, or both in the same way that "Christianizing" was an initial justification for imperialism. Even before World War II, when imperialists had control of much of the world's resources, leaders of the imperial powers such as Great Britain, France, the Netherlands, and Belgium began talking in terms of "development." This term meant both a kind of organized economic reform and additionally one that would involve making women more productive, their work more lucrative, and the economy in general more modern. At first development was to benefit the imperial powers; now it benefits the new, independent governments with women working in multinational companies or in agriculture or craft work. Development programs bring in funding from agencies interested in women and can increase tax revenues.

In the last few decades global agencies of many kinds have worked to promote development and especially to focus on women's role in development in order to alleviate their poverty. The idea behind these programs is often that women in Southern regions are backward, abused, or economically inactive. In Africa, for example, the history of outsiders misinterpreting women's role in the economy is a long one and generally ignores women's economic creativity and the centrality of their knowledge to food security. Despite this, the statistics of women's poverty, which result from their insecure position in society more generally, have convinced such global organizations as the United Nations and the Ford Foundation, not to mention an array of national and local NGOs, to put money into the development of women's capacities. Governments are not slow to seek out these funds by themselves picking up the call for women's advancement in the economy. Women's improvement is said to promote democratization, a goal of many of these global bodies, and becomes, as mentioned, not only a justification for foreign activism but even for military invasion.

One especially contested part of the recent development agenda has been the sponsorship of microcredit or microfinancing, often arranged by NGOs, philanthropists, and businesses. Microcredit involves lending small amounts of money to individual women and men—though most often women—to establish a small business such as making prepared food to market or performing services such as beautification. The program of microcredit has allowed some recipients to be successful in pulling themselves out of dire poverty and giving them a sustainable livelihood. Critics of the program point to the thousands of others who remain not only in poverty but in debt because they have no training in business, market conditions are not good, or the recipient does not have the requisite wherewithal to sustain an enterprise. Moreover, critics say, microcredit puts unfair pressure on individuals without much training or adequate backing to overcome all the handicaps of entering the big world of capitalism where the forces against individual success are overwhelming. Like much of development, microfinance is a program devised and run by outsiders, perpetuating the overwork and poverty of women in the Southern regions of the world. For critics, then, it is just another aspect of neo-liberalism.

ORIENTALISM AND ITS CHALLENGES

There is a long history of such a focus on women in Asia and Africa and it has produced exotic or emotionally charged images of women in developing countries. This is one enduring legacy of colonialism, often called "orientalism." The term is applied to Western paintings of women in the harem; the concept of "orientalism" was studied in writings just after World War II but popularized by the critic Edward Said. The idea of orientalism contends that Western scholars wrote about people and societies in the Middle East and studied their languages as a way of obtaining the power to dominate foreign lands through knowledge. In this way of thinking, knowledge itself is a power, and one made special use of by the growing study of the Middle East as an "other"—that is, a non-Western place, culture, person, or group of people. Women's Studies makes us consider that the non-Western woman is a special kind of "other."

Said and his followers writing either about oriental "others" and orientalism as power over those others were not especially interested in women and gender. Most of them missed the fact that much oriental knowledge was presented as knowledge of the harem and as displays of the sexuality of Middle Eastern women and later of African and other Asian women. Western artists painted oriental women as either nude or seductively dressed as objects of sexual desire, placing them in erotic backgrounds such as baths. Authors fantasized about them in their writings as mysterious—meaning highly sexed and shrouded in bodily secrecy. Harems were regularly imagined in almost pornographic terms, while the woman in the harem represented all that was "other" about the Middle East— especially its supposedly oversexed culture in contrast to the supposed rationality of the West. Only recently have scholars written more objectively about life in the harem, sometimes describing the agency and even power that women exercised.

There have been many responses from local women to the orientalist construction of women and to the neglect of considering the gendered nature of this construct. The study of actual women's lives and the presentation of women's voices have served to highlight this neglect. One sees active Middle Eastern women taking charge of their lives and destiny. Life in the household or in the workplace becomes vivid in testimonials and in fiction. Yet there is a paradox in that the heightened production of such testimonials and the discovery of facts about Middle Eastern women serve to produce the same kind of knowledge-power that anti-orientalists criticize. This knowledge can actually fortify the Western sense of superiority as different patterns of life become clearer. Difference that was once imaginary in orientalist eyes becomes a cornucopia of facts. In other words, it could be said that the study of women only enhanced Western power because so many of these studies were written by Western scholars—in this view orientalism continues in Women's Studies scholarship in the West.

Others have presented ways of Middle Eastern life in a local setting in order to capture the specificity of local ways using local categories that might not have relevance to the West. Young women in Istanbul, for example, describe their religious faith in these terms: "We pray like you have fun." They attend films with religious values and spend their spare time in group devotions or performing charity work. The West is not a point of reference but instead the daily routines and values of other young Turkish people they know are the focus of their comparisons. Women's Studies works to uncover the specificities of local cultures from a vantage point beyond orientalism.

It is seen, nonetheless, that reference to the West and to its projection of the "oriental woman other" is inevitable, not only in the desire to escape the West but in the very production of women in modern times. At the beginning of the twentieth century, Chinese reformers, wishing to become more like the West and thus more modern, invented a term for "woman." Before that, there had been words for wife, mother, sister, aunt, grandmother, and other female relations but not one for women disconnected from the family and its organization. The idea was that the West had such a word and that reforming the condition of women was key to becoming modern. The first step was actually creating a category of woman distinct from the family—one who was an individual, rational in her own right, and capable of developing as an autonomous human. In order to have an autonomous woman all sorts of other changes needed to take place: for instance, a Chinese woman's feet needed to be left in their natural condition instead of bound, child marriages had to be outlawed, and the life-and-death hold of the family patriarch needed to be relaxed. Development programs have used this focus on making women modern to advance their own agendas.

In this reading of globalization and feminism, we seem hedged in by Western hegemony to the extent that all feminism can be interpreted as the product of men's drive for a Western-style modernity. Nonetheless, Women's Studies has taught us to look for a less restrictive reading of hegemony, always looking at points where an undoing of paradigms and supposedly logical truths occurs. In the case of Chinese feminists, they were able to work their own interpretations and create their own uses of modernity. Even slight moves can be seen as signs of struggle with larger forces that seem to hem women in or construct the conditions of women's existence for them.

WOMEN'S GLOBAL SUBJECTIVITY

Many accounts see women in global society as crushed by their overwhelmingly difficult life situations. For one thing, the power of patriarchy and capitalism are omnipresent; in economic terms the result is women earning ten percent of the world's income and owning only one percent of the world's property. Women's poverty, in turn, endows patriarchy with its wealth and power. On the cultural level, the fact that so many work in domestic and other personal service work also feeds an image of women workers as domestic—rooted, that is, in the home instead of the public sphere where power is located. In this system, however, the global economy can be said to offer jobs—either at home or as migrants—to women in poor countries where they traditionally have had little economic opportunity. It is in the context of these jobs and the macroeconomic forces that shape their inequality that women find myriad ways of maneuvering through migration, living on the margins of the law and otherwise building sustainable lives for themselves and their families. They build skills and subjectivity.

We see fictionalizing globalization and the imperialist past as the kind of subjectivity formation that women workers also exercise. Post-colonial writers display the kind of sensibility that also works to weaken colonial, patriarchal, and capitalist claims. Post-colonial writers have had trouble with critics in their own lands accusing them of writing in the style of their former masters when they adopted poetic forms and the narrative novel to make their observations of the world. They had become too Westernized, the criticism went, and ignored indigenous values and forms. Many celebrated women novelists such as Botswana writer Bessie Head and Nigerian émigrée Buchi Emecheta told the stories of their lives in conventional novel form. Both often expressed disillusionment and confusion given their own strivings to make good and become successful. Thus it was seen that imperialism remained both in the culture at large and within the individual writer. Simultaneously these writers' confusion has displayed a multiplicity of interpretations and a questioning of situations that opens up debate and shatters monolithic readings.

Other authors have worked to alter the circumstances of their lives and to seize control of narrative through fiction. From the 1980s on, the Latin American boom in literature and its "post-boom" featured several women writers of real accomplishment. Given the overwhelming misogyny of male writers and their celebrity in the global literary market, these authors worked in a macro-economic climate of novels that were hostile to women and proudly patriarchal. Writing in the genre called "magical realism,"

Chilean author Isabel Allende wove larger-than-life male characters whose violence against women across generations was shocking. Her *The House of the Spirits* (1982) was translated into many languages and sold some 60 million copies, in defiance of the Chilean dictatorship and oppressive male privilege. Allende received death threats and eventually moved to California, operating in a global world of menacing politics just as her characters experienced global economic exploitation and sexual abuse. Although Allende could not transform the macropolitical situation or the larger social conditions in which she lived, she struggled with these, thus altering her own subjectivity.

The list of women authors from around the world is endless and their work takes many forms. Nobel Prize Laureate Rigoberta Menchu's testimonial to the conditions of Native American life in Guatemala during the 1970s and early 1980s was different still from conscious works of fiction. It gathered together the community's experience of oppression, including starvation, imprisonment, torture, rape, and murder, and presented it to the world in *I, Rigoberta Menchu*. This testimonial to Quiche life and her own coming to activism celebrated the worldview of her people as they endured the forces of racism, capitalism, and military dictatorship. Amidst this story, Menchu describes her own development of an activist sensibility when she witnesses the rape and torture of women from another Indian ethnicity. From then on she devotes her life to achieving justice, no matter what the cost. Women's Studies uses these and other writings of thousands of women writers across the globe as examples of women's subjectivity.

GLOBAL FEMINIST ACTIVISM AND MODERNITY

The process of achieving democracy through women's political activism, as well as their integration into a modern economy, can also bring support and funding. Because of this global goal of promoting democracy, especially through agencies of the more prosperous North, states have come to advocate for the creation of feminist movements, often for middle-class ones, in many emerging nations. Guatemala, for example, could support middle-class women activists, although not Menchu, because attention to the former brought international funding. The case of Morocco is also instructive in this regard. In 1992, the newly elected government backed a "One Million Signature" campaign devoted to mobilizing the Moroccan citizenry to back women's rights—both political and personal. Moroccan women were already active on their own behalf, but the backing of the government as part of national modernization and advancement made a big difference. Additionally in 2000 the government sponsored a big march in support of the National Plan of Action for Integrating Women into Development, which was proposed to the national assembly. This law would modify family law as embodied in shari'a, Islamic law of family, personal, and other relations in order to bring them more in line with Western "universal" law. Because the campaign made no acknowledgment of respected values in the society, it provoked a counter-movement by other women to protect their status under Islamic law.

Women have organized groups loosely categorized as non-governmental organizations or NGOs and the results of this activism have been seen as both harmful and beneficial. There are women's NGOs, for example, in North and sub-Saharan Africa working to stop the genital cutting of girls (a topic we look at later). Because these NGOs undertake to change local practices critics interpret them as meddling in people's lives as an offshoot of earlier imperialist interventions. The aim of imperialist reformers was to make other parts of the world more "Western" and "modern" in their daily lives and present-day activists are often criticized for these reasons. However, NGOs can also empower women to enter politics to change social behavior that is harmful to them and their children. After the fall of the Soviet empire, global NGOs provided training and resources so that women would be strong enough to participate in politics and thus ensure that the transition to democracy would not be an all-male event.

Brazilian women living in urban neighborhoods of shacks called favelas have also organized themselves, setting up systems for eliminating the garbage that city sanitation services ignored. They also instituted night classes where they learned to read and where volunteer workers facilitated their brainstorming about their situation both as women and as poor people with family responsibilities. Political self-emancipation was their goal. Nobel prizewinner Wangaari Mathei encouraged women to work with her to plant trees to reforest areas around the Kenyan capital, Nairobi. Mathei gathered funds so that women could be paid for this work even as they had a personal investment in not seeing the area regress to desert. Mathei's work elicited resistance from corrupt politicians who wanted to siphon off all contributions and foreign aid funds for themselves. They so threatened her life that Mathei temporarily fled the country in order to be safe. These examples of activism of many kinds in different parts of the world provide lessons for Women's Studies globally, especially lessons in the complexity and paradoxes of activism.

Finally, women have practiced activism transnationally, across national boundaries, and this global activism has enriched its participants and all who study women-centered politics. From national movements that circled the globe from the end of World War II onward, interconnections among women grew. The first postwar undertaking took place with the beginnings of the United Nations where women met internationally to ensure that the United Nations and its founding documents specifically addressed equal rights for women. They composed the UN's Commission on the Status of Women—a commission the women delegates had lobbied to have made independent of a commission on rights. Their efforts were realized in the preamble to the Charter of the UN, which stated a commitment to "fundamental human rights, in the dignity and worth of the human person, in the equal rights of men and women." Although women from the United States have been given all the credit, it was actually those from Latin America and Eastern Europe who spearheaded these early meetings, successfully drawing attention to issues important to women at the same time that they established a political profile on the international stage.

As feminists revived their presence in the politics of their individual nations in the 1960s, the slogan "Sisterhood is Global" arose. There was pressure for the United Nations to declare a "Year of the Woman" and to host an international conference. The first of these took place in Mexico City in 1975 and was part of a series of conferences that together constituted the UN's "International Decade of the Woman." What became clear at that meeting was the comparative backwardness of women from "developed" countries when it came to understanding global issues. Taking themselves as the norm, they were ignorant of what was going on in the wider world, as confrontations at the meeting demonstrated. Activists appeared committed to a far wider array of issues than were women from the so-called "First World" and from that activism there emerged the true beginnings, according to many, of a truly global agenda—one created by the world's women and not by those who identified with the powerful West.

CONCLUSION

We will continue to investigate, compare, and contrast Women's Studies issues from around the world in subsequent chapters. So far we have laid out some founding issues of the Western Women's Studies tradition and those that have had a more global resonance such as Marxism and issues of class, racial, and ethnic difference. Colonialism and the imperial past have left their mark on much of the world in the form of racialization, violence against women, and their exoticization. All of these have left women vulnerable to the forces of global capital, albeit with many paradoxes. All the while exploiting women, global structures push them into prominence as the world's victims, justifying overscrutiny and many forms of intervention. Women become the project of national modernizers, international NGOs, and even military adventurers whose tanks, bombs, and drones are supposed to "save" them. Nonetheless, post-colonial women create their own subjectivity as authors, activists, workers, migrants, and politicians, adding to the complex understandings of Women's Studies students and researchers.

SUGGESTED READING

Lourdes Beneria, Lourdes (2003) *Gender, Development, and Globalization: Economics as if People Mattered*. New York: Routledge.

Bose, Christine E. and Kim, Minjeong (eds.) (2009) *Global Gender Research: Transnational Perspectives*. London: Routledge.

Ching Yoon Louie, Miriam (ed.) (2001) *Sweatshop Warriors: Immigrant Women Workers Take on the Global Factory*. Cambridge, MA: South End Press.

Dutt, Malika (2000) "Some Reflections on United States Women of Color and the United Nations Fourth World Conference on Women and NGO Forum in Beijing, China" in Bonnie G. Smith, *Global Feminisms since 1945*. London: Routledge.

Menchu, Rigoberta (2010) *I Rigoberta Menchu: An Indian Woman in Guatemala*. Elizabeth Burgos-Debray, ed. Ann Wright, trans. 2nd ed. New York: Verso.

Mohanty, Chandra (2005) "'Under Western Eyes' Revisited," in Elizabeth Lapovsky Kennedy, Agatha Beins, eds. *Women's Studies for the Future: Foundations, Interrogations, Politics*. New Brunswick: Rutgers University Press, 72–96.

Ong, Aihwa (2006) *Neoliberalism as Exception: Mutations in Citizenship and Sovereignty*. Durham: Duke University Press.

Magalit Rodriguez, Robyn (2010) *Migrants for Export: How the Philippine State Brokers Labor to the World*. Minneapolis, MN: University of Minnesota Press.

Ngai, Pun (2005) *Made in China: Women Factory Workers in a Global Workplace*. Durham: Duke University Press.

Roy, Ananya (2003) *City Requiem, Calcutta: Gender and the Politics of Poverty*. Minneapolis, MN: University of Minnesota Press.

Roy, Ananya (2010) *Poverty Capital: Microfinance and the Making of Development*. New York: Routledge.

Smith, Bonnie G. (2000) *Global Feminisms Since 1945*. London: Routledge.

Speed, Shannon (2007) *Rights in Rebellion: Indigenous Struggle and Human Rights in Chiapas*. Palo Alto, CA: Stanford University Press.

Wang, Zheng and Ko, Dorothy (eds.) (2007) *Translating Feminisms in China*. London: Wiley-Blackwell.

5

WOMEN'S STUDIES AND THE QUESTION OF GENDER

The word "gender" circulates everywhere these days. Terms like "gender gap," "gender-bending," and "gender bias" are all currently part of our common vocabulary. The term arose almost simultaneously with the globalizing of Women's Studies and in many people's eyes it has posed a challenge to Women's Studies. In fact, for the past 20 years, people have often talked about Gender Studies rather than Women's Studies and some universities have even changed the name of the major to Gender Studies. The idea behind gender is that it is not enough to study women as a unique group to come to a true and useful understanding of women's situation—including their past and present condition. Rather, one needs to take into account men's lives as well; the entire male–female organization of a society, a family, or a workplace contains essential information. One cannot simply investigate women to understand violence, economic inequity, or the place of women in political processes; the field of gender relations holds the key to the situation of women. To some extent this recalls the assertion in the early days of Women's Studies that women could not be understood outside the context of the family because women's identity depended on the rules, norms, and context of family life. Most matters pertaining to women's identities unfold in some form of male–female relationship, including the overall values of society when it comes to

masculinity and femininity. For some that relationship may constitute an important duality that is a basic building block of the
world. Women do not stand alone.

Beyond the assertion of gender's relevance, however, definitions
of the term are highly variable. The most common understanding
of gender among the public is that it is a substitute for the term
"woman". Among people in the academy, some take the term to
mean that the social facts of men's roles as "men" are important to an
understanding of the social facts of human organization generally.
Studying gender entails describing men and women equally. That
is, we need more information about men as a sexed group, not
merely as the major human actors who are only accidentally men.
Men's Studies has thus come to be a growing undertaking in the
university. A second definition asserts that to understand women
we must understand how men's and women's roles as sexed beings
relate to one another. Because men's roles in society have involved
so much power, their activities naturally influence the roles of
women and their overall status. In this interpretation, the charge is
to dig down into the operations of men as men in their overall
attitudes towards themselves and the privileges they exercise over
women and children. Finally, gender is also an idea or category that
emerged from many different fields of thought including post-
structuralist, anthropological, and literary theory. Around it developed additional terms such as "binary" and "universalism," which
have provided the term gender with new meanings in many
Women's Studies classrooms.

Given all these varying definitions of gender that this chapter will
explore, what are the plusses and minuses apparent in using that
term to date? Critics maintain that gender takes away the interest in
women because men are seen as endlessly fascinating due to their
power and privilege. In short, for critics, the study of gender merely
reinforces the status that men have held in society and in university
curricula by shining the academic spotlight on them one more time
only from a different angle. Additionally, as we shall see, the term
"gender" is also seen as a category devised by white Western feminists to discuss the power of their men, with whom these women
are at odds. Instead of the solidarity between men and women
based on oppression found outside the West, scholars of gender put
an overemphasis on division, albeit in the context of a common

gender system. Finally there are some who find "gender" too restrictive and unresponsive to identities that are fluid, passing between male and female and even surpassing those categories.

Despite such criticism, some will claim that gender has been a major breakthrough for Women's Studies researchers and students as well as for scholars in many of the university's more traditional fields. Why is it that from New York in the United States to Kazan in Russia programs in Gender Studies are seen as advanced in comparison to an outdated feminism and a "weak sister" discipline—Women's Studies? These questions suggest that there are plusses, breakthroughs, and negatives we can associate with the term gender. Before coming to any conclusions about the role of gender in Women's Studies, we need to dig deeper into its many definitions and to examine its usefulness to date.

CURRENT DEFINITIONS OF GENDER

Gender has marked the way men and women dress and behave, determined the spaces in which they conduct their lives, and awarded the power that they wield in the family and wider world. Some critics say that the word "gender" was once a grammatical term indicating whether one used a gendered pronoun or adjective before a noun and that it is a misuse to consider it to describe society. Additionally, before the concept of gender became so complicated that it set off debates in the university, gender meant sex roles and often sex segregation. In the modern world men have generally earned more money than women have, enjoyed more privileges because of their sex, and held the major political offices locally, nationally, and internationally. These conditions have been attributed simply to definitions of appropriate sex roles, it is often said. The higher positions and greater privileges of men in the entire modern period are currently aligned with the fact that masculinity is more highly valued than femininity because of the operation of gender norms that have shown remarkable resilience over time. It is their role to be more powerful and valued in contrast to women's perceived lesser value. Nonetheless, in the past 200 years women have come to contest male privilege and the arbitrariness of the greater value given to men that has resulted in women living in greater poverty, working harder, and enduring domestic and other violence simply because of their sex. The rise of feminism as a form of activism contesting gender definitions or sex roles has produced some modification in the political, economic, social, and cultural power men hold because of their gender. With the sex roles definition of gender, all that is needed is a reform of society so that equality reigns. It is a simple political task to change sex roles and the way they operate in society.

Are there other ways of looking at gender? As mentioned, the term gender is commonly used simply to refer to women: thus, gender gaps and gender history have come to mean the way women vote and earn money or the behavior of women throughout history. Most people think "women" when they think "gender." Many academics, however, use the term in another way: to refer to the differences between men and women, usually understood as leading to different roles for each sex and to differentials in power and influence. Gender in this usage is about the cultural hierarchy that makes men more valued than women and not simply about beings labeled "man" or "woman." Some scholars have viewed gender as the primary human difference, determining for example who gets a good job, receives health care, and enjoys personal security. Others suggest that the determining factors in human history and in current social conditions depend on the intersection of gender with other factors such as race, ethnicity, class, sexuality, and religion (see Chapter 4 on intersectionality).

Another main ingredient of current gender theory is the idea that the differences between men and women are constructed or artificial. This understanding began with the global work of anthropologists such as Margaret Mead, whose books from the 1930s and 1940s described societies in which men performed what Western society would see as "feminine" tasks and women performed so-called "masculine" ones. Mead pinpointed the many variations in men's and women's roles globally, leading to the conclusion that gendered behavior was determined by custom rather than by nature. The philosopher Simone de Beauvoir provided a second buttress to a slowly emerging theory of gender when she wrote in her 1949 bestseller *The Second Sex* that "One is not born, one is made a woman." From then on, there was steady intellectual movement toward uncovering the artificial nature of all gender distinctions. That is, the interrelated behaviors of men and women—or "gender"—were not natural; they were cultural and constructed by human society and human beliefs.

Thus Simone de Beauvoir's *Second Sex* was a crucial moment in advancing more relational ideas about gender as a fabrication. This dense and lengthy description of the "making" of womanhood discussed Marxist, Freudian literary, and anthropological theories that, according to de Beauvoir, actually produced women's behavior. In her view women, in contrast to men, acted in accordance with men's view of them and not according to their own lights. This analysis drew on phenomenological and existential philosophy that portrayed the development of the individual subject or self in relationship to an object or "Other." Thus, as de Beauvoir extrapolated from a variety of thought, a man formed his subjectivity in relationship to "woman" as other or object, spinning his own identity by creating images of someone that was not him. Instead of building selves in a parallel way, women accepted male images of them *as* their identity. By this view, femininity as most women lived it was an inauthentic identity, although said to be a natural condition. For Simone de Beauvoir it was the result of a misguided choice to accept someone else's construction of their being. This insight had wide-ranging implications for future Women's Studies research, notably in pointing to a woman's sexual role or nature in terms of its "constructedness."

A second idea deriving from existentialism in *The Second Sex*, however, touched on women's biological role as reproducer. For French existentialists, living an authentic life entailed escaping the world of necessity or biology and acting in the world of contingency and uncertainty. From this thinking, as we mentioned, de Beauvoir stated that women were additionally living an inauthentic life to the extent that they just did nature's bidding by having children and rearing them. They should search for freedom and authenticity through meaningful actions apart from biological necessity. The assertion that women could escape their biological destiny to forge an existence apart from the family also opened the way to gender theory by detaching femininity from the body. What were women—and for that matter, men—if not beings somehow rooted in innate and inescapable biological characteristics? A group of translators in the Northampton, Massachusetts, area working under the aegis of H. M. Parshley made *The Second Sex* available to a widespread Anglophone audience in the 1950s, with the project as a whole arousing great excitement in the Smith College community. Small wonder that Betty Friedan, Gloria Steinem, and other Smith alumnae and students at the time were among the pioneers of the second wave feminist movement.

GENDER, STRUCTURALISM AND POST-STRUCTURALISM

De Beauvoir's was not the only French doctrine to lay some of the groundwork for gender theory. During that same postwar period the author Claude Lévi-Strauss claimed in his structuralist theory that people in societies lived within frameworks of thought that constituted grids determining everyday behavior. These frameworks were generally binary, that is consisting of oppositions such as pure and impure, raw and cooked, or masculine and feminine. Binaries operated with and against one another as relationships. One could and did draw from structuralism that in the case of masculine and feminine, these concepts or characteristics were mutually definitional. Lévi-Strauss developed these theories in *The Elementary Structures of Kinship* (1949), in which he took kinship as the fundamental organizing category of all society. Kinship, Lévi-Strauss insisted, was based on the exchange of women. The American anthropologist Gayle Rubin elaborated on Lévi-Strauss in "The Traffic in Women" (1975), an article that further developed gender theory again using French concepts as its basis. "The subjection of women can be seen as a product of the relationships by which sex and gender are organized and produced," Rubin wrote. Her second point, derived in part from Lévi-Strauss, was that the most important taboo in all societies was the sameness of men and women. By 1980, it had become commonplace in US anthropologists, sociologists, and some psychologists in academe to talk about "the social construction of gender"—that is, the fabrication within these structures of sexual difference. To quote a 1978 textbook, "Our theoretical position is that gender is a social construction, that a world of two sexes is a result of the socially shared, taken-for-granted methods which members use to construct reality."

Rubin's article also highlighted the work of French psychoanalyst Jacques Lacan, who emphasized the symbolic power of the phallus, the relational nature of the masculine and feminine psyches, and the nature of the split or fragmented subject in even stronger terms than Sigmund Freud had done. Freud had seen the rational, sexual, and moral sectors within the self as in perpetual contest. Rather than being whole, the psyche or self was fragmented. In an essay on the "mirror stage" in human development, Lacan claimed a further, different splitting. The baby gained an identity by seeing the self first in terms of an "other"—the mother—and in a mirror, that is again, in terms of an "other." Both of these images were fragmented ones because the mother disappeared from time to time, as did the image in the mirror. The self was always this fragmented and relational identity—and one that was always searching for wholeness. Lacan also determined language to be a crucial influence providing the structures of identity and the medium by which that identity was spoken. In speaking, the self first articulated one's "nom" or name— which was the first name of one's "father"—and simultaneously and homonymically spoke the "non," the proscriptions or rules of that language, which Lacan characterized as the laws of the "father" or the laws of the phallus. Lacanianism added to gender theory then developing in the United States a further sense of the intertwined nature of masculinity and femininity, beginning with identity as based on the maternal imago and fragmented because of it. Second, it highlighted the utterly arbitrary, if superficially regal, power of masculinity as an extension of the phallus and its symbolic authority over the human psyche. Third, the fantasy nature of the gendered self and indeed of all human identity and drives received an emphasis that became crucial to some practitioners of gender history.

All of this is difficult material, but we believe that it is worth wrestling with because it is the foundation for some forms of gender theory. Under what came to be known as "French feminism," French theorists picked up on Lacanian, structuralist, and other insights to formulate a position that contributed to the development of a certain kind of gender theory in the United States and parts of Europe. For theorists such as Luce Irigaray, masculine universalism utterly overwhelmed and obstructed feminine subjectivity—in other words, the status of women depended on masculine pronouncements said to be universal truths. What Simone de Beauvoir called "the Other" had nothing to do with women but amounted to one more version of masculinity—male self-projection. Women thus appeared as erasure, as lack, and in Irigaray's *This Sex Which Is Not One*

(1985), as unrepresentable in ordinary terms. The woman was the divided, nonunitary, fragmented self while men represented wholeness and the non-sexed. The logical outcome of such thinking was to throw Women's Studies in its many variations into question. For example, the historian of French women and labor Michelle Perrot compiled an anthology titled *Is a History of Women Possible?* (*Une histoire des femmes est-elle possible?* 1984). The idea behind the question was that given the absence of a unitary, definable female self, could there be a history or anthropology or sociology of "women"?

We will not go into the influence of Michel Foucault on theorists of gender, except to point to further steps along the path of seeing gender as enmeshed in a grid of power that produced subjects or individuals called male and female according to the way in which they enacted the rules of sexual difference. Such power was political, originating in state and social rules. Flowing through populitons and bodies, this power is called biopower. Foucault's work showed bodily behaviour not as determined by biology but as participating in biopower in the performance of sex and gender roles. It dismissed the traditional sense of humans having autonomous, individual selves—an emphasis that was extended to the development of other aspects of gender theory, notably the idea that gender and sex are not about biology but about performance.

JOAN SCOTT: GENDER: A USEFUL CATEGORY

Although many of these theories had more or less influence on the sociology, anthropology, and social history of women by the mid-1980s, in 1986 they came together when the historian Joan Scott issued her stirring manifesto about gender theory in the *American Historical Review*. Scott asked American historians to transform scientific, social scientific, and positivist understandings of gender by adding insights from Lacanian psychoanalysis and from Jacques Derrida's deconstruction that showed the difficulties of assigning definite meanings or truth to texts, and Foucauldian–Nietzschean definitions of power. In her view Marxist, anthropological (aside from those of Gayle Rubin on which her own theory depended), and psychological moves toward understanding gender had reached a dead end because they assigned to the terms male and female essential and enduring characteristics usually derived from biology.

Nor, for that matter, according to Scott, were feminist scholars who studied patriarchy or sought out "women's voices" on steadier ground. Despite great progress, even those who now followed the lead of "binary oppositions" of structuralist anthropology had no convincing way of accounting for men's oppression of women. The rigidity of the male–female categories in any of these systems, especially in the work of those who sought out women's "voices" and "values," kept gender from being as useful as it could be.

As a corrective, Scott considered the way the use of this trio of French theorists could help overcome the rigidities and insufficiencies of gender theory as it had evolved to the mid-1980s. Lacanian psychoanalysis rested in part on the Swiss linguist Ferdinand de Saussure's understanding of language as a system in which words had meaning only in relationship to one another. It coupled this insight with revised Freudian ideas about the psychic acquisition of identity as a process shaped by the supremely high value placed on the phallus. It was this relational value that the symbolic system of language expressed. For Scott, Lacanianism and all the psychic variation it involved were keys to understanding gender as a demanding, inescapable relationship. Foucault's theory of power as a field in which all humans operate offered another valuable insight. Scott suggested that using Foucault allowed for the introduction of gender issues into political history, because gender itself was a form of power derived from creating and manipulating binary differences—primary among these being the difference that created men and women. Understanding gender in this way allowed for history, sociology, anthropology, and other disciplinary elements in Women's Studies to analyze politics because it was around the difference called gender that politics was organized.

Scott explained that gender could be a category or subject of discussion through which power operated. It could operate thus in several ways. For one, because gender meant differentiation, it could be used to distinguish the better from the worse, the more important from the less important. Using the term "feminine" articulated a lower place in a social or political hierarchy no matter what the term referred to. Gender explained or assigned meaning to any number of phenomena, including work, the body, sexuality, politics, religion, cultural production, and an infinite number of other terms. As such, phenomena were coded male or female, or as debates within these fields deployed categories of masculinity and femininity, power was at work. Thus, thinking about gender was a way to think about power, whether in society or in politics.

More recently, Scott has taken the position that gender theory is about understanding difference broadly conceived. As she explains, gender especially helps us address the functioning of the mysterious thing we call sex difference. In this definition, gender is less about men and women and their lives than about the uses of difference (or gender) in structuring a society, assigning power, regulating behavior and shaping politics. In this version, gender becomes truly a useful category because it teaches all of us to think about difference and its mobilization in society at large. As mentioned in the case of gender, this mobilization of difference can affect both the enormous realm of politics and the personal life of the individual and of couples. At its heart gender is about the play of difference from the time that the baby ponders it in relationship to his or her parents, and all of this is terribly mysterious. In maturity one can be at the mercy of the forces of difference as they pervade people's lives, causing not just confusion but even neurosis or rage.

Sexual difference or gender in Scott's most recent works is so powerful because it touches on the fantasies that have developed since childhood over sexuality and identity. Our identities progress through the tortured processes of becoming a sexed adult. We know that politicians gather their power by talking about gender and sexuality—whether that has to do with birth control, teen pregnancy and teen irresponsibility, abortion, hetero- and homosexuality, and many other topics that stir all the repressed fears and desires located in our psyches and in the public psyche. Gay marriage is a prime example of the way difference is emotionally charged and used for political purposes. We may long for the mother's breast or the father's male power symbolized in the phallus; we may have unacknowledged fears of castration and other forms of sexual lack. All of these desires and fears are susceptible to political and other manipulation but also to analysis through the study of gender.

GENDER STIRS UP THE UNIVERSITY

It should go without saying that although the category "gender" is tossed around freely in ordinary talk, gender still stirs up debate.

Because gender deals with issues of fear and desires centered on sexual difference, it can be a highly emotional topic to discuss. Moreover, many of those discussions can be based on varying interpretations of what gender means. We cannot even begin to cite the thousands of works that have subsequently been published in the United States using weak, strong, misunderstood, and utterly twisted versions of gender theory as it emerged from Americans' encounter with France. Nor is it the purpose of this chapter to examine all the debates over America's engagement with France or to name all the people engaged in this important transfer of knowledge that continues down to the present, including the ongoing theoretical turns and refinements of both Scott herself and Judith Butler. Moreover, there were other important French thinkers such as Frantz Fanon who further contributed to ideas of difference and an understanding of intersectionality in gender theory. Currently there is much discussion of circulation, routes, and pathways of knowledge, and it seems to me that the development of gender theory around the world—as is now the case—from this French–American connection should be explored in depth by all students and faculty as one of the most powerful examples of that circulation in present times.

Arguments against gender and gender theory are legion. Joan Scott's definition of gender, as it has been adopted across the world in both strict and looser ways, elicits controversy and even outrage. The idea of gender as necessarily locking men and women together as part of an analytical couple seems to erase the entire history of feminism, which was very little about men and very much about validating and valuing women on their own terms. That outrage stems from the implication and even the outright statement that the category "woman" on its own is not really useful and thus that feminism is not useful. People in Women's Studies have often made the claim that their field revolutionizes knowledge; moreover, they feel that theorists of gender would deny the value of their work and the vast strides the study of women over the past 50 years has made. Gender delegitimizes them as well as the entire field. So far in this book we have shown some of the important breakthroughs—the basics—on which such claims rest. However, those supporting the term "gender" suggest that adhering to traditional definitions of "women" or "woman" as an autonomous being endowed with rights that need to be upheld is a throwback to seventeenth-century ways of thinking and that it will never undo sexism.

In other words, those who adhere to the gender theories of Scott and others charge that the category "woman" as traditionally defined and studied both by women writers centuries ago and by feminists and scholars today will never push the boundaries of thought and political activism. All one has with the category woman as it has been used for centuries and then taken up by Women's Studies scholars and activists as a subject of reform or even revolution leads to the tired impasse of equality versus difference, universalisms versus particularity. In this latter case, the universal category of rights, which was only ever meant to apply to men, cannot be transformed by discussing women's rights, although specific situations may be rectified temporarily. Those rights will never meet the "universal" standards growing out of a line of thinking that says that rights apply to all. Women's Studies has neither produced real change nor undermined male domination. Understanding the psychic hold of difference as embodied in gender, many believe, holds such a promise.

Critics of gender theory strike back by calling it unrealistic in its rejection of real women's needs. Gender theory talks about categories, representations, and binaries. It appears to make light of the poverty in which so many live, the violence they suffer, and the limited human rights—including the right to food, health care, and safety—they enjoy. Those wanting to preserve the primacy of "women" in Women's Studies point to the need for more statistics, facts, organization, and activism on behalf of real women. Gender as it evolves theoretically is too abstract and disembodied when one looks at the state of women around the world—making up with their children some 80 percent of the people living in abject poverty.

Besides that, other critics say, the post-modernist idea of gender as devised by US and European theorists is set up as a universal, something that applies everywhere and to all people. There are places in Africa where neither names nor language are gendered in any way relevant to the linguistic side of gender theory. Difference is mainly structured around age, as is power. But Westerners focus on the body and see in it difference between men and women, using the categories of gender and sexual difference to exert intellectual hegemony over other knowledge workers around the world. In fact, people in the West have created both Women's Studies and feminism, using them in the spirit of an intellectual neo-imperialism as they focus on women—something that is irrelevant to African ways of thinking and knowing.

Apart from this lively attack on both the categories woman and gender, there are strong preferences for focusing on women instead of gender. Another major defense is that the category gender is diluting the study of women and increasing the study of men. Scholarship has always been mostly about men, the criticism of gender goes. With the category gender the scholarship on men under the guise of "gender studies" has been "rebranded" to include the study of men as "men"—that is as gendered beings. Do we really need more studies of men when books such as *The Body in Pain* had one sentence on women's pain (in childbirth) and hundreds of pages on the pain of the soldier and on men generally under torture? Added to that is the case that since the launch of the idea of gender as an important category, one offering more insights and opportunities than studying women, those who study men as gendered beings are gaining a great deal of traction in the university and among publishers and even students. Books on men's consumerism, men's bodies in wartime, male sexuality, men's health, the psychology of masculinity, and a vast number of other topics proliferate to the detriment, the accusation goes, of scholarship on women. With "Gender Studies" seemingly more important than Women's Studies, it often seems to some in Women's Studies as if we are back to square one. That is, studying men remains far more important and exciting than studying women, who throughout history and down to the present have been less valued as subjects of literature, sociology, history, and the arts.

SEX VERSUS GENDER

There are still more discussions centered on the term gender. Another that comes up is unpacking the difference between gender and sex. Some accept the idea of gender as a "construction" of sexual difference that is separate from the biological "reality" found in the body. In other words, gender was about expectations, ideas about men and women, and artificial regulations for men and women to set clear, if artificial, boundaries between the sexes. Gender referred to prescriptions for behavior according to whether one was a man or a woman that might have nothing to do with practicality. Gendered prescriptions were simply a way of dividing up the social pie—not an absolute recipe for making that pie. Whereas the pie needed specific ingredients and a recipe in order chemically to succeed, cutting it up did not operate according to any precise or predetermined conditions.

In other words, gender did not operate according to necessity but operated according to socially created formulae. Sex, however, was another matter, many believed. Still adhering to a more or less "biology is destiny" creed was the idea that while gender was constructed, biological sex was "real" and palpable. It was something that could not be denied and actually determined who was male and who was female. Even the idea of the "five sexes" used chromosomes and physical characteristics to decide upon a so-called "real" sexual identity, expanded though the number of those sexes might be. No one, the argument went, could escape biological sex while one could play, it was thought, with gender.

In what has become a muted battle over gender versus sex, the philosopher Judith Butler has taken the side that both gender *and* sex are culturally determined and defined. The person of whatever sex, she argues, is hollow of intrinsic meaning as to their biological definition, for biology itself is a human formulation. In actuality, the person is thrown into culture at birth, following all its rules and regulations that pertain to what that person's sex is said to be by the humanly constructed science we call "biology." The person, then, is a being upon whom the defining rules—created in the human field called biology—for determining sex behavior are imposed just as the rules of gender come as a human formulation or formula. There is nothing *essentially* either male or female biologically or culturally. Such names are all assigned qualities, characteristics, and behaviors by society, including biologists, teachers, police, legislators, and parents. One then performs sex and gender according to the rules that are covered by such names as man, woman, girl, boy, daughter, son, and so on—all of these are biological/sex and gender terms and all of them "constructed." Sex and gender are equally acts or performances of the rules surrounding all those assigned names.

TRANS PEOPLE AND THE UNWINDING OF GENDER

For centuries there are those who have transcended gender categories. In Southeast Asia, those who defy conventional male/female definitions or who move from one category to another in a variety of ways have long existed. Across the globe, such people operate in a transgendered way by adopting the clothing and stereotypical behavior of another sex, while others take hormones or have surgery to change their anatomy. Still others deliberately blend identities, looking somehow genderless, in which male and female are not easily distinguishable. Those transcending gender in one way or another have been seen in some societies as workers of miracles or holy and as belonging to a "sacred gender." Still, even within the practices of moving back and forth across a border between the sexes, some maintain that the idea of gender remains, if only implicitly as a norm that is defied.

Trans people in the West are often those who have used hormone therapy and surgery to achieve gender neutrality or to move from one sex to another. The idea for many is that they have been born into the wrong sex or in some delineating sex identity that confines them to a single gender role and an attendant set of strict gender expectations. In the United States, the first person to acknowledge surgical procedures to change physically from one sex to another was Christine Jorgenson, a US man who went to Europe in the mid-1950s to have sex-reassignment surgery. Once a woman, Jorgenson became a media sensation, someone who rocketed to fame because of this transformation. Jorgenson herself was eager to live a normal life as a woman, but for many years the press and the public could not let go of her story. This was because, while not breaking the taboo of gender sameness, she had broken another one against gender and sex being fluid, temporary, and indeterminate. Christine Jorgenson, opinion-makers and society at large worried, had been born male and was now by most norms female. What did this mean for sex and gender? Didn't it obliterate their clarity beyond what theories of sex and gender did? We will continue to discuss trans people, but for the moment it is sufficient to ask whether their lives and practices don't throw gender and sex into question more than theories do.

CONCLUSION

Gender is a complicated category and there are several definitions of it. The commonplace use of the term is as a synonym for women. Another is simply to add men to the topics for consideration in Women's Studies. The idea is that we need to know more about men in order to understand the condition of women in society and to figure out relationships of male power and female subservience. Still another way of seeing the value in adding men to Women's Studies is to consider that we need to see men as gendered and sexed human beings in order to have the full range of gendered and sexed behavior to work with in our thinking. Understanding that range and the variability in gendered and sexed behavior will again enhance the field of Women's Studies' insight. Finally, the definition of gender as difference is an important one because it allows us to think abstractly about what those differences mean in the creation of power around them. People's fantasies of wholeness or their need for there to be clear sex differences can be and are used politically. Seeing gender as difference in all its complexity gives us a great deal to think about.

Gender as a category and ruling concept has provoked intense debate of many kinds. One of the most powerful questions is whether the concept of gender will drive out the study of women. At virtually no time in history about which we have documentary knowledge have the status and well-being of women not been under attack. Women's Studies has made understanding women's status and well-being its central focus. There is thus the concern that under the category of gender the study of masculinity will reduce and already has reduced the focus on the study of women because men are seen as more important and noteworthy. There will be far more studies of men than there will be of women and we will be back where Women's Studies started—that is, with no provocative studies of women. This is another reason why Women's Studies scholars outside the West see gender as a "nicer," "liberal" category that overrides more hard-hitting studies of women—on their poverty, illiteracy, and the violence directed against them.

Despite criticisms and concerns, today Women's Studies has incorporated "gender studies" practices and ideas by looking at women relationally and by factoring in the interactions among defining concepts for the sexes. In addition we look at the ways in which those interactions and definitions produce power or are the products of social and political power. In sum we can say with confidence that concepts of gender are all to the good because they expand our tools and enrich our analyses. Many dismiss Women's Studies on the grounds that it is too much about arousing emotions so that women feel good about themselves. Others say that it is just women's politics. The debates over Women's Studies versus Gender Studies have shown that this is a terrain for intense thought and major intellectual controversy.

SUGGESTED READING

Chaudhuri, Maitrayee (ed.) (2004) *Feminism in India*. New Delhi: Kali for Women.

Connell, Raewyn (2009) *Gender: A Short Introduction*. 2nd ed. Cambridge: Polity Press.

Halberstam, Judith (2005) *In a Queer Time and Place: Transgender Bodies, Subcultural Lives*. New York: New York University Press.

Oyew'umí, Oy'erónké (2005) *African Gender Studies: A Reader*. New York: Palgrave Macmillan.

Meyerowitz, Joanne (2002) *How Sex Changed: A History of Transsexuality in the United States*. Cambridge: Harvard University Press.

Rubin, Gayle S. (2011) *A Gayle Rubin Reader*. Durham: Duke University Press.

Scott, Joan (1999) *Gender and the Politics of History*. Rev. ed. New York: Columbia University Press.

FEMINIST THEORIES AND METHODS

There are many "theories" that now inform Women's Studies and methods that are called "feminist" or distinct to Women's Studies. The theories are sets of ideas clustered together as part of unified, systematic thought such as "critical race theory" or "post-colonial theory," both of which we have alluded to in earlier chapters. Theories may be said to be in contrast to early feminist ideas, which, some theorists suggest, were merely criticisms of society's treatment of women in a standard rather than revolutionary way. That is, Women's Studies sociologists or economists paid more attention to information about women's lives than was usual for their disciplines. Still, their findings were based on normal "positive" or fact-finding activities to which both male and female scholars subscribed. Neither feminism nor Women's Studies in the eyes of theorists could really work change because they were so piecemeal and normative, aiming at reform rather than a transformation in thinking. Feminist theorists acknowledge the importance of giving voice to inequities but they suggest that mere criticism of men, society, or values produces little movement to a better place. Violence against women persists despite feminism, this line of thinking goes, as does women's inequality. Feminism did not raise the status of women: despite decades of activism and more recently Women's Studies research, women continue to be generally seen as less valuable and less worthy than men. Feminist theories developed with the idea that deeper or holistic analysis was needed. Such theories were wide-ranging in their approach, quite varied, and some of them even mutually antagonistic. Taken together, they show the way in which Women's Studies generates new knowledge and ways of looking at the world.

We reflect that Women's Studies began with feminism as the strongest point of its analytical base. Feminism had evolved over the centuries in the West as a quest for equal rights including rights to education, to sovereignty in the body, to vote, and to have a good job. It wanted women to be held in equal regard to men as well as gaining equality in political, economic, and social conditions. Parliaments, workplaces, and the home were to be transformed as places where women had the same status as men. Outside the West, pro-women thinking and activism concerned many of these same issues, but there was an additional, concerted emphasis on the right to basic needs such as food, shelter, clean water, good medical care, and freedom from bodily harm, especially after the downfall of colonialism left many regions of the world stripped of their resources and struggling for well-being. There was also in the activism of women in post-colonial nations an emphasis on analyzing the continuing exploitation from countries of the North and a much greater solidarity with men. Structures of power were at the center of investigation and theorizing for many. All of these points of analysis have developed even further down to the present day under the Women's Studies umbrella but some of them began as theories quite distinct from concerns for reforming gender inequity.

Theories involve transforming one's way of thinking, providing new tools for critique, and seeing the activities and representations of women from fresh perspectives. They can also involve thinking about gender and difference broadly and more conceptually. How Women's Studies carries out and thinks about its procedures is another aspect of theory, sometimes seen as gendered as in the term "feminist epistemology" and at other times connected with distinctly pro-women ways of investigating women's lives and presenting findings, as in the term "feminist methodology." We will look at arguments for theory, present several specific theories that have been both influential and contested, and examine the development of what is called feminist methodology.

WHY THEORY?

Some scholars argue that more is needed than activism and the traditional analysis of statistics and other social facts to make sense of the conditions that women face. They suggest that students and activists need theory to guide their thinking and to solve problems. Ideas arranged in an organized form can often provide and provoke novel solutions to burning issues—old and new. In other words, theories are what some people use "to think with," as the saying goes. Theories are seen as handy equipment, part of a "tool kit", or even as provocative ideas that spark the flames of inquiry. Those outside of Women's Studies engaged in such endeavors as grassroots organizing have used theories—for example, of how power operates in unseen ways or how gender prejudice can be invisible yet forceful. A human rights activist, working to ensure food security and clean water supplies among the poor in the United States, claimed that "I use theory all the time in my work."

How can this be so? How can sets of ideas, some of them seemingly "highfalutin" or detached from real problems, be useful? Skeptics seeking practical answers to women's oppression can legitimately ask how theory can help students and activists. As we have seen, the mere word "theory" can raise objections and even make some people angry. It can seem extravagant and even useless to talk about the world of ideas when hard-headed solutions are needed. Often theory appears elitist, available to those equipped with its special language and familiar with philosophical concepts. In fact it may seem to go against the Women's Studies model of activism where the aim is to draw in people from all walks of life and empower them with useful knowledge.

Is it true that theory is only made for people with a special language and a very high degree of education? We think there is value in learning about the range of theories that have informed Women's Studies so that you, the student, can have the benefit of knowing about and even mastering some of the most widely used theories. People who know about theory simply have more options when thinking about women and devising solutions to problems. Theory can be seen as beyond our everyday concerns for the world's people to benefit from clean air and sufficient food. Admittedly, theory seems, on the surface, to be of little use to activists working to end violence toward women. Some activists, however, see that theory offers them something motivating and expansive rather than something that ties them in knots. Isn't it a good idea, some of them will say, to wrestle with tough theoretical ideas as a way of sharpening thinking skills and developing tools for critique? Moreover, because it often comes from a perspective different from the activists' point of view, theory can provoke new ways of thinking that those engaged in Women's Studies have always welcomed. Learning theory can provide an awakening or it can challenge our beliefs in positive if difficult ways.

We consider it important to present some of these theories in their basic form so that readers can decide for themselves if these theories can advance their thinking. We also suggest that some people who reject all theories are actually operating from a theoretical position— one so familiar to them that they can't see they are using it. It is often important to understand theory so that we can become aware of our own (perhaps unexamined) theoretical assumptions. Although we have referred to many of these theories as part of the development of early Women's Studies, let us take a fresh look at their meaning today and consider a sampling of the theories available to people and often of importance in Women's Studies classes.

FROM MARXISM TO POLITICAL ECONOMY

Marxism at its heart is a critique of capitalism, and in today's world a critique of global capitalism. As such it can appeal to those in Women's Studies who oppose capitalism as oppressive of women— and additionally of many men. Marxist feminists see issues of equal rights for women and minorities as simply unattainable under capitalism—a pipe dream perpetuated by good-hearted but deluded liberals. Many women outside the West believe Western scholars to be such misguided folk because they regard rights rather than global economic exploitation as the root of women's wide-ranging unequal status. As Marxism evolved under an explicitly feminist analysis, women were seen as the perpetual servants of capitalism, the ones who could be infinitely exploited by the language and functioning of capitalism. Taking care of their children and the home, women today are interpreted as the mainstays of the current capitalist economy by reproducing and guarding the next generation of workers. In addition, as part of this role, women are capitalism's chief consumers, who advance the circulation of goods and the massive profits to those who own the means to produce those goods. Thus, women are both the motor of and grease for the capitalist system according to a Marxist Women's Studies perspective. Karl Marx himself hardly reached this level of understanding of women's centrality to capitalism, but over a century later the analysis of this dominant economic system has achieved new levels of sophistication once the exploitation of women is seen to be the foundation of capitalism's health.

In some cases, Marxism has given way to the field of political economy, a study that seeks to find the political interests and operations behind the workings of the economy. Those who observe the situation of women from the position of political economy argue that mainstream feminism in the West, especially as it is articulated by white middle-class activists, fails in its mission to benefit women. Instead it merely exhausts them, for in addition to the gritty problems of being chief consumer and child rearer, feminism demands that women take a role in the workforce and in the public sphere, both of which only add to their burden. Perhaps, political economists charge, middle-class feminists can afford to offload the jobs that are part of the cultural expectations for women: nannies can care for children and personal shoppers and housekeepers can handle consumption and home upkeep. Capitalism affords few women such options, however.

Specifically, working-class women under capitalism labor to exhaustion. As for women in the rest of the world, capitalism's spread as part of the system of colonialism already exploited women in all these ways, only with longer workdays and even harsher working conditions. Whether in the countries of the urban North or in those of the more rural South, there is no escape from capitalist exploitation. Moreover, the needs of profit-making industries have recently combined with neo-liberalism, which holds that social services connected to the welfare state and even expenditures for education and health care of workers can draw resources away from innovation and economic growth. Seeing business people as the most valuable to society as a whole, neo-liberals want profits to be high and taxes on those profits low because profits will eventually "trickle down" to make jobs that benefit those who need work.

The income of workers and the well-being of the poor is less fundamental to overall social good than high profits and low taxes on wealth. For many who look at capitalism from the perspective of analyzing an overall political economy, neo-liberalism, now a prevailing view around the world, is a policy that once again works against the interests of ordinary people—especially women. Combined with Marxist analysis, the inevitable outcome is capitalist oppression as neo-liberalism increases the burden on women by cutting back on social services and even their children's access to education. In Marxist theory, there is no way out for women except the overthrow of the capitalist system. Unlike Marxist feminists a century ago, few expect this to happen even though new political movements have begun targeting banks and other leading capitalist institutions.

Marxism's current view of the economic situation of women worldwide is a major change, in large part due to the rise of Women's Studies. Feminist Marxists and scholars drawn to Marxist economics have give Marxism both a more concerted focus on women and a more targeted look at the way in which capitalism is an interlocking and hierarchical system of gendered production. This global analysis has come to see capitalism as having specifically regional inequities and gendered ones where women's unpaid and lower-paid work is essential to profit. Global capitalism also pits ethnicities against each other, all the while recently announcing businesses' commitment to multiculturalism, which allows such comparisons to be made. One wonders nonetheless if the end of the exploitation of women and others that Marxists predict to follow the end of capitalism would in fact occur. Those countries that are non-capitalist or have been non-capitalist have generally continued to relegate women to unpaid reproductive labor, to the lowest-paid jobs, and to a social status that is inferior to that of men. Most non-capitalist countries have had massive hierarchies of male leaders. Despite this, Marxism continues to provide a theory persuasive to many in Women's Studies.

PSYCHOANALYSIS

Psychoanalysis is still a powerful and attractive tool for some thinkers, even as it has evolved and remained highly criticized in our own day. So, let us review and dig a little more deeply into Jacques

Lacan's theories first, and then look at feminists' use and adaptation of them, including their differences from the master. Lacan had thought-provoking ideas, first among them the "mirror stage" in the formation of any personality. This occurred in infancy, when a child, identifying with the mother as part of his or her self, found her absent when, for example, she stepped out of the room. This so-called splitting of the self caused distress, even trauma, and produced the search for wholeness that usually lasts a lifetime. But seeing itself and thus finding an imaginary wholeness, the child gets a sense of mastery and thus constructs an ego that allows for human functioning, including the accomplishment of tasks and participation in the wider world.

Second, there is the complicated issue of the phallus in the forma-tion of any identity. The phallus, a symbolic figure, represents desire and power, which briefly put is associated with the male. It is not, however, the actual penis but representational and something that figures both male and female desire. The importance for feminist thinkers was that men figured themselves or were figured as the phallus—or the embodiment of power—while women lacked the phallus and wanted it or to be desired by it. Third, the power of the phallus as activated in the power of language. The grip of the symbolic phallus and the grip of language combined to create an inescapable structure of unequal power in our psychic make-up. We cannot escape because of the patriarchal world of language into which we are born. One needs to recognize the grip of language and that the world we think we are creating independently and in full freedom is an illusion—a world that is already created for us in language dominated by the phallus. We are all trapped in its power.

It is at this point that French and other feminist theorists entered psychoanalytic-philosophical debates, sometimes in a way that was difficult to comprehend for those used to the clear, straightforward demands of feminist activists. The major contribution of these French feminist theorists was to show the inner complexity of people's lives, suggesting—if not in explicit terms—that life and gender roles are more problematic than those political positions working for equal rights and justice for women have claimed. For example, if the phallus as symbol is so powerfully embedded in our society and our individual psyches, how is it that anyone can expect this power to disappear? Those who think legislation will simply create equality are deluding themselves, as history in the twentieth century has shown. For a century activists claimed that the vote would eliminate bias against women. Despite a century of equal rights legislation, the power of women remains small, and their salaries in relation to those of men equally so. Theorizing the operation of phallo-logo-centrism—that is, the concentrated power of words and masculinity—aimed to explain the perpetual power of men and ended up with rather pessimistic answers because it places us in an inescapable position. Yet it is this psychoanalytic perspective that gives us a more realistic sense of what activism is up against. In fact, many feminist theorists criticize both Marxist and especially Freudian theories as overwhelmingly misogynist for seeming to normalize male power and to get women to agree that their situation is hopeless. Those women who don't agree are seen as filled with rage rather than rationality. They are said to be consumed by penis envy and other disagreeable qualities such as neuroses and psychoses, on display when they resist the internal power of patriarchy in the psyche.

Moreover, the power of the phallus works at the psychic level, as we have suggested in the mobilization of people's emotions over issues of sexuality, gender, and difference. Understanding the symbolic fear of castration described by Freud and of the loss of wholeness described by Lacan should open doors for interpreting a range of gender issues. French feminists for example have tried to escape what seems a dead end in the inevitability of phallic power by focusing both on women's desire—sexually and even politically—and on women's status as "lack." They validate women's sexuality and pleasures. Another answer is that the quest for wholeness and for the missing mother (who remains in our psychic make-up) can lead to feminist movements and goal-oriented activism. So, the fantasy of reuniting with the mother and making the self whole is a powerful one. Simultaneously, feminist theorists talk about "*écriture feminine*" or women's writing as a way to disturb the phallic control of language and as a way to explore women's subjectivity and even patriarchy itself. If our individual personhood comes into being through language, then understanding women's place in language and their use of it is key to feminism. The idea was to explore and even validate sexual difference in language in order to upset male control of it and thus of order.

RACE THEORIES

Some people accuse Women's Studies of implicitly taking white women as their default subject and priority. This is for the most part true because whiteness as a "universal" was globalized with imperialism, slavery, and colonization. White feminism still resonates and often remains either a celebrated or criticized point of reference. Simultaneously, extraordinary thinking about race abounds, and there is a pushback against whiteness. For one thing, from the outset of the contemporary women's movement, some black women theorists rejected the term feminism as having little to do with their lives; instead they followed the lead of African-American author Alice Walker who proposed "womanism" as an alternative. Walker's definition of womanism included the words courageous, lover of the spirit, and lover of women or men, suggesting an exuberance amidst struggle on the part of black women. Another early point of criticism among scholars of color involved in race theories is that few other theories take race into account—psychoanalysis, Marxism, and critical theory, to name just a few. Sometimes the excuse of the creators of these theories is that "we can't cover everything," while others simply find race uninteresting—both of these reasons also given for not including gender in analyses. African-Americans initially composed one group of scholars who rejected theory on the grounds that it had little to do with their lives either as blacks or as women. Theory, the idea went, is elitist and impractical. It treats of fancy words and concepts that appear in the form of jargon, when there are serious and looming problems stemming from regular discrimination in people's lives. Evelyn Brooks Higginbotham, however, challenged African-American women and other women of color in the academy to step back and consider what theory could actually do for their thinking.

In fact, there is no lack of theory among women of color, black women, women of mixed race, and among those interested in race as a category on its own and especially in intersectionality. One of these is the theory of racialization. This is a term from race theory, and it involves the processes that cause people to become aware that they are seen as a raced "other." This may involve being seen as "black" in the United States, as a mestizo or mulatto in Latin America, as Chinese in New Zealand, and as an aborigine or indigenous in a

variety of other countries. Racialization comes about because the identity as the "other" is an identity that screams inferiority, and another
blind spot for whites is that they are unaware of their own racialization
and its privileges because they are the norm. Racialization itself is an
especially haunting and harmful condition, especially given current
political ideologies that claim the equality of all people. For
Women's Studies theories of racialization connect with those of
sexism to create intersectionality, but intersectionality that considers
the fusion and internalization of several inferior identities.

Mestizo women such as the Chicana, lesbian poet and theorist
Gloria Anzaldúa have sometimes attempted to turn multiple
racializations into a virtue. While poetizing about the pain of
racialization, she simultaneously sees her multiple identities as
fracturing attempts by society at large to racialize her accurately.
The inaccuracies and stereotypical moves that the dominant race
makes to racialize allow her room to establish her own self, even as
the pain of racialization is inescapable no matter how aware she is
of its inaccuracies.

Black scholars have also created standpoint theory—another
major set of ideas that influences Women Studies. It holds that
African-American women have had unique experiences that they
work into different kinds of knowledge. The production of
knowledge along with their special experiences constitutes their
standpoint, which in turn informs and produces politics. Patricia
Hill Collins describes the knowledge resulting from that experience
as a legacy of struggle against racism and sexism. The example often
given is of Sojourner Truth, the US slave and activist, who spoke of
her work in the fields, the use of her muscles, and the conditions of
her motherhood as shaping who she was and what she knew. But
one black woman's standpoint will differ from another's, often
shaped by social class, sexuality, and ethnicity, for example. The
idea of a "woman of color" eradicates that specificity; some
African-American women insist upon their "blackness." The goal
of black women's thought is to arrive at embracing a self-defined
standpoint, one that is created despite but because of the actions of
white society to delegitimate black women intellectuals' theories.

Among some black theorists there is at once an acceptance of
feminism that is melded with African-American liberation and a
broadening out to a position that aims to eradicate all forms of

domination. The latter is espoused by the theorist bell hooks and also by current thinkers who seek a way to bring together those who would and do live outside the structures of power stemming from heteronormativity and white patriarchy such as the state, family, and work. Contesting all categories, theorists of this form of liberation take their cues from two main sources: "women of color feminism and queer of color critique" (Kyungwon Hong and Ferguson 2012: 1–24). The Combahee River Collective inspired the idea of "women of color feminism" for showing the ways in which black women dropped out of social concerns. When black women were murdered in large numbers, the authorities treated those deaths as an insignificant loss, members of the Collective pointed out. Theirs were lives not valued. Queer of color critique allows for the dissolution of all identifying categories such as gay/straight, black/white, upstanding/criminal, and the like and rejects the need for a person to become a striving, heteronormative member of society. A fusion of multiple positions, the black woman is released from her intersectional devaluation by denying the utopian belief in acceptance, achieving, and belonging. This position has links to the postmodernism that we will discuss next. Suffice it to say, these theories reached by thinkers in Women's Studies and elsewhere across the university are both innovative and challenging, as we have come to expect from our field of thought.

POST-MODERNISM AND WOMEN

Post-modernism has developed from or is related to some of theories we have already discussed. Suggestions in psychoanalysis that our psyches are neither whole nor rational but rather fragmented and shaped by "irrational" drives has led postmodernist theorists of the self to see the individual as not having a distinct, integrated, and whole identity. As psychoanalysis threw into question the "modern" faith in the autonomy and rationality of the individual and even the status of the supposedly "real world" in which we live, post-modernist thought also questions older ideas of our rationality. Instead, post-modernist theory suggests that the individual is not an autonomous actor making rational choices about her life course, but rather that there is a set of behaviors that are followed as part of living in a society structured by laws and norms. Each

individual, being born into this set of norms, is thus already pro-
grammed, as the rules produce the individual and as the power of
the rules flows through her. There is no "originality" in a person's
character or internal life but rather the performances of powerful
rules in thought and deed. As one performs rules, one empowers
them and simultaneously performs their power.

Scholars in Women's Studies have been at the forefront of
developing post-modernist theory. For example, as mentioned in
Chapters 3 and 5, some see gender identity as a performance of
rules and norms and they reject as impossible the quest for rights as
a cure-all to male privilege and domination. There is no female self,
nor is there a masculine one, so the drive for individual rights does
not really make sense when the autonomous, rights-bearing individual is simply a norm never designed for women in the first place.

However, there are problems with Women's Studies as well,
according to post-modernists. The priority given to women or to
gender always puts other categories—race or class, for example—in
second place, as women of color were the first to spot. Because of
this and because of the incoherence of the idea of women except as
a set of performances, isn't it time to rethink having Women's
Studies or Gender Studies? Such a critique has helped usher in a
type of thinking called "queer theory," which would eliminate the
proliferation of categories associated with whiteness, heteronormativity, sexual or other identity, and so on. In other words, the
idea in queer theory (which we will discuss more in Chapter 7) is
to eliminate all the forms of identity that facilitate the development
of hierarchy. While some embrace what is called identity politics of
women, gays, trans, or blacks, queer theory, as it has evolved to the
present, calls for a rejection of all such identities.

We want to look at another side of post-modernism that
Women's Studies has embraced and that is its playfulness, imagination,
and irreverent positioning in dominant cultures. Post-modernism in
the arts does away with originality of style, often merging an array
of styles in a building or painting. Styles in post-modernist art can
also be whimsical, satirical, or downright mocking and funny, when
it comes to dealing with the "high standards" of art and everyday
behavior. Women artists have excelled at post-modernist creations,
as is evident for example in Nikki de Saint-Phalle's colorful statuary
and Haitian artist Rosemarie Deruisseau's whimsical depiction of

Voodoo. US artists Barbara Kruger and Cindy Sherman are renowned for their satires of women and American consumer culture.

POST-COLONIAL THEORY

The end of global empires brought independence to former colonies and the formation of many new nations. At first leaders of these movements were concerned with the shape of new nations and promoted thinking in terms of nationalism. As we have seen, some thinkers such as Frantz Fanon addressed the problem of the liberated self in light of what colonialism had meant to everyday existence and identity. Whereas Fanon thought in terms of "decolonizing the mind," these new thinkers coined the term "subalternity" to describe the colonial condition. Subalternity was initially a military term indicating an inferior member of the army, usually a lower officer or ordinary soldier. Because many theorists of post-colonialism were South Asian, the term arose naturally from the masses of South Asian men and others who had served in the British army.

Although those who served under colonialism have been called subalterns, colonized people and citizens of formerly colonized regions who are now independent are now included in that category. The idea is that subalternity is an enduring condition, even down to the present. People remained subalterns long after colonization not only because their economic situation had not truly become free from colonial domination but because the individuals still lived in a colonial culture where Western values were seen as the only important ones and where they still resonated in people's minds.

Post-colonialism involved cultures that were impregnated with feelings of inferiority to the "master" cultures and their values. The idea was that such impregnation made it impossible for subalterns or former subalterns to speak of themselves, of their desires, and of most other things except in the voice of the masters. However, the theorist Gyatri Spivak carried the position further to point to women as a special category of subaltern, even as the subaltern of the subaltern. "Can the subaltern (as woman) speak?" Spivak asked. Assuming that she can't, white women have for several hundred years, the charge goes, chosen to speak on her behalf.

Western women have rushed to investigate the special situation of the subaltern woman and even to serve as her ventriloquist under imperialism and post-colonialism. They seek to elaborate on and analyze the subaltern position of non-Western women in their books, speechifying, and activism, which makes for another form of silencing. Simultaneously, the Western woman—whether teacher or scholar—gains voice and confidence. She points in detail to the abuse of "Third World women" and cites their poverty in evidence. She elaborates the violence against those women fated to live outside the West as part of their degraded condition. In this way the position of the Western woman is enhanced, as her own verbosity adds verbal degradation to the silencing scholarship and activism that have worked against the subaltern. The Western feminist, it has been charged, swells in stature in these interactions with the subaltern of the subaltern. Colonialism continues in the guise of feminism.

What has emerged, not only from feminist activism outside the West but from scholarship, is a picture of the Third World woman as uniformly debased, a portrait mirroring the justification for colonialism in the first place: that women were treated badly by bestial Third World men and that they needed rescuing. Gyatri Spivak pointed out that this silencing of the variety of women's voices marked another aspect of women's subalternity—and, we can add, it still shapes Western understanding of the non-West. The *Time* magazine cover showing an Afghan woman whose nose had been cut off as punishment exemplifies this idea, offered up as justification for US intervention in Afghanistan from 2001 onwards. Afghan women, the justification went, are so abused that they need rescuing from barbaric men and from their own debasement. Colonial theorists might argue that while welcoming the voices of subalterns would not necessarily yield the "whole truth," it might have undermined the claims of military, capitalist, and other agents of colonial and post-colonial power to be philanthropic in their goals. Subalterns might not see themselves as utter victims but they also might see themselves in this way.

Searching for the multiple voices of subaltern women can involve the new and diverse readings of such cliché-ridden, ideologically powerful, and women-centered events as sati, the widow immolating herself on the funeral pyre of her dead husband, or other examples of widow suicide. Whereas these have heretofore been given firmly negative interpretations concerning the brutality of Indian men and the gender regimes they enforce, readings informed by post-colonial studies find multiple reasons for such acts, including an agency on women's part with multiple and not always certain components. Other suicides of women are now interpreted not romantically but as acts with more uncertain motivations. In other words, post-colonial readings of women's subalternity serve to break down monolithic stereotypes. As mentioned earlier, readings of Muslim women's uniform oppression when they wear headscarves has now similarly been found to have multiple motivations. When it comes to women as subalterns, a new and more informed focus on their situation and agency has led, as we have seen, to an understanding of the ways in which unpacking their multiplicity can unmask colonialism's ways. It can also reveal their own subjectivity.

A similar issue comes with genital cutting, which we examine in a later chapter on sexuality. In general Western society has long been outraged by this practice and called it genital mutilation. But this is to serve as ventriloquists for the colonized and formerly colonized women and girls. Even if these women were to speak, post-colonial theorists ask, what would be shaping their words? Post-colonial theory powerfully reminds women around the world to consider the position from which they speak and the impact of colonialism on that speech. Insofar as North–South inequities still loom large, these post-colonial inequities should play a major role in Women's Studies analysis.

METHODS, EPISTEMOLOGY, AND ETHICS IN WOMEN'S STUDIES

How we think, investigate, and write about subjects is tied to our methodology, our epistemology or ideas about knowledge, and our ethical commitments. Our research and writing may be positivist— that is, wedded to official information, scientific procedures, and statistics, for example. As mentioned earlier, this methodology has been sharply criticized for employing precisely those tools that have been used against women. The activist poet Audrey Lorde challenged all Women's Studies and Race Studies practitioners when she warned that "the master's tools will never dismantle the master's house." These tools include the so-called reason that feminist moral philosophers have found so wanting because they discount and even scorn the knowledge embedded in emotions such as anger and fear. It challenges the tool of confidence that men's scholarship in the past has been neutral, producing only truth. Proponents of traditional scientific methods also discount the knowledge that standpoint theory finds so important for women and minorities. Scientists would find this knowledge lacking credibility and reliability because it is personal and perhaps even unique to one person. We do not, seeing instead that claims to neutrality and objectivity are statements to effect intellectual domination.

Over the decades, Women's Studies has in fact produced new ways of thinking and writing that fall under the umbrella terms of feminist methodology and feminist epistemology. On the most basic level, feminist methodology challenges the verifiability and universal truth in writings produced according to the scientific method. It finds many of these findings partial and the product of male privilege and commonly held ideas about women's inferiority. An additional critique is that traditional researchers look at those they are studying from a position of power, allowing them to interpret and even overwhelm their subjects with those interpretations. Ethnographers who study other cultures have been accused of claiming to "go native" and befriend their subjects as part of their procedures. These acts dupe those who are being studied and seem to continue the process of imperialism with their falsehoods and power plays.

Feminist methodology and epistemology call for new attitudes and approaches. Right from the beginning, Women's Studies valued women's experiences and writings as few had ever done before. After that, researchers examined the actual situatedness of women's lives and worked their way through the sexism that distorted research methods and abstractions that misstated the world in favor of masculine biases. It questioned all existing approaches and representations of women, as we have tried to do, for example, in Chapter 4, where we look at the paradoxes in portraying the impoverished woman, including her use as a money-raising tool and as an excuse for military invasion. Women's Studies researchers and students thus take the best from the traditions of the sciences, social sciences, and humanities and work to identify sexist procedures, biases, and conclusions. It does this by looking at the communities of researchers in the past and their practices as scholars and networks of scholars. The individual feminist researcher now understands her own work as enmeshed in a web of psychological, social, and political conditions and influences.

Simultaneously, Women's Studies has come to value the words of women even as they come forth in researcher–woman situations. That is, instead of emphasizing first and foremost the researcher's objectivity and rationality, the value comes from the subjectivity of the women themselves as part of the study. Thus, Women's Studies uses many approaches in its methodology. Although it values science and objectivity, it likewise values the words that spring from those being studied. Using a multitude of approaches, one can also factor in the social constructedness of what is being articulated. Recognizing the multifaceted nature of women's lives, Women's Studies uses an array of methods, some of which we have touched on in this and earlier chapters: objective investigation, theories, testimonials, concepts of gender and social constructedness, and many others. Should, at some point, a single and uncomplicated methodology emerge from Women's Studies, it will be all to the good. For the moment, Women's Studies methodology flourishes both as practice and as debate.

CONCLUSION

Women's Studies as critique and cutting-edge thinking is alive and well, especially in its engagement with theories and its concerns for methods. Women's Studies teaches us to look at the theories held by others with respect and to consider that there are different methods for coming to truths. We talk in terms of truths or a truth, not *the* truth, for we learn that there are multiple truths, some of them competing and even paradoxical; so that while we are always concerned with methods in arriving at a truth, we are aware that there are a variety of methods and an array of findings. Nor is everything in Women's Studies in line with our beliefs, some of them fervently held. For example, theory has helped us understand that using the term "woman" has its own problems. It can imply racism and classism, appear to support the global North over the global South, and omit the harms done to men outside the charmed circle of power. Hard-won theories have brought us to these sometimes painful, sometimes divisive understandings. Multiple theories and the clash of findings are all to the good and that is why we have presented them both in this chapter and over the course of this book. Being informed and having a well-stocked tool kit of intellectual tools advance the field.

SUGGESTED READING

Butler, Judith (2006) *Gender Trouble: Feminism and the Subversion of Identity*. New York: Routledge.

Gray White, Deborah (2008) *Telling Histories: Black Women Historians the Ivory Tower*. Chapel Hill, NC: University of North Carolina Press.

Kyungwon Hong, Grace and Ferguson, Roderick A. (eds.) (2012) *Strange Affinities: The Gender and Sexual Politics of Comparative Racialization*. Durham: Duke University Press.

Lewis, Reina and Mills, Sara (eds.) (2003) *Feminist Post-Colonial Theory: A Reader*. New York: Routledge.

McCann, Carole R. and Kim, Seung-kyung (eds.) (2010) *Feminist Theory Reader*. 2nd ed. London: Routledge.

Negy Hesse-Biber, Sharlene (ed.) (2012) *Handbook of Feminist Research: Theory and Praxis*, 2nd ed. London: Sage.

O'Shaughnessy, Sara and Krogman, Naomi (2012) "A Revolution Reconsidered? Examining the Practice of Qualitative Research in Feminist Scholarship." *Signs*. Vol. 37. No. 2 (Winter 2012).

Peterson, Spike (2003) *A Critical Rewriting of Global Political Economy*. London: Routledge.

Spivak, Gyatri (2010) *Can the Subaltern Speak? Reflections on the History of an Idea*. New York: Columbia University Press.

Wallach Scott, Joan (2011) *The Fantasy of Feminist History*. Durham: Duke University Press.

EMBODIMENT AND SEXUALITY

In the 1990s sexuality emerged as a defining aspect of Women's Studies, although there were clear calls from the feminist movement for exploring the subject before that. Since then, sexuality has remained at the forefront of issues that we study and debate, expanding to encompass the broad category of embodiment. Sexuality can mean behaviors and desires; for many it can also refer to an individual's announced identity as straight, gay, or bi. Women's Studies classrooms engage in debates over "identity politics," with sexual identity featuring prominently among the other identities under consideration. Whereas once sexual identity and sexual behaviors motivated political activism to gain equal rights and to protect each individual's sexuality from discrimination, today sexual identity can generate activism stressing pride and the cultural assertion of that identity. Embracing the term "queer"—once a scornful and negative word—is one example of the far more positive and more complex understanding of sexual identity including the right to have no sexual identity whatsoever.

Since Adrienne Rich's coinage of the term "compulsory heterosexuality" appeared in 1980, courses have developed with sexuality as their exclusive theme, as in "sexuality studies." Rich's characterization of heterosexuality as compulsory and forced challenged the field to rethink all sexual practices and norms. Later, queer theory also added to the richness of sexuality studies and can even be said to surpass normative investigations of sexuality. Queer Studies has come to constitute the subject for entire courses rather than a supplement to investigation of sexuality more generally. Queer theory undoes some of the older rights-based activism and some of the earlier insights of sexuality theory. It provides a fresh, more fluid, and some say more generous vision for discussions because it tends to deny the existence of a "normal" sexuality and normal embodiment of any kind against which everything else stands as abnormal. It also throws Women's Studies into question in very fruitful ways—even leading to the idea that we are in a "post-feminist" era (a concept that we will consider at the end of this work).

Sexuality joins a focus on the body more generally—whether it is a reproductive body, a heterosexual body, a trans body, or a non-normate—often called "disabled"—body. In speaking of the body, the tendency is toward simplicity and matter-of-factness. People will often see the body as determining one's gender, sexuality, and the pattern of one's life. Others, in contrast, will see the body as a "construct," lacking a determining materiality or physicality. That is, our bodies in all their aspects do not determine us; rather, we act out bodily rules and follow representations in our dress, demeanor, work life, and other behaviors. The study of embodiment in Women's Studies is thus full of complexity, even though people may think of it as exceedingly simple and self-evident.

Disability Studies offers still another, though far less glamorized, way to approach investigation of the body, as it calls into question the implicit domination of the "normative" body studied earlier in Women's Studies scholarship. Our lived world is built to favor certain body types and every social practice and value privileges the fully able-bodied. The disabled are regularly aborted or if not they often live impoverished and discriminated against in a variety of ways. Thus, sexuality and the body pose issues central to political interests and scholarly ones. Although students are still concerned with reproductive rights, with which much of the work on sexuality began, we now have a wide range of new terms and new subject matter to cover—all of them encompassed under the rubric of sexuality and embodiment.

GENDER AND BODY POLITICS

The body has long been the subject of political control, debate, and activism. In terms of political control the female body has been regulated by custom and law about the places where it can take up residence: for instance, in France, the Napoleonic Code of 1803–4, which influenced laws worldwide, stated that a wife legally had to reside where a husband decided she should live. In Prussia the husband was the arbiter of the time a mother devoted to breast-feeding. Legal systems around the world have regulated the sexual disposition of a woman's body, mandating the age at which a female could have sex and marry and regulating her fertility in myriad ways. We review at greater length these practices of bodily regulation in this chapter.

Women's bodies have also been the focus of exaggerated spee-chifying, as in the sanctification of the maternal body in fertility cults, Christianity, and other religions and the demonization of sexual expression in such forms as masturbation and prostitution outside official regulations and customs. Yet amidst this we think of women under colonialism and the many ways in which they used their bodies as political tools. For example, in 1928 in the Aba Women's War, Ibo women from the region that is currently Nigeria mustered rituals from their traditional repertoire to protest new taxation being imposed on them. They removed their clothing, painted their bodies, carried leaves and branches, and demonstrated before officials who were carrying out the order to tax women. The body was shown to be a political tool and one that deployed sexuality in the name of achieving power. Other African women practiced scarifica-tion that often carried an erotic message for their sexual partners. Under imperialism, they also used this bodily adornment as a sign of anti-imperial pride, seeing in their unique bodily designs an emblem of nationalism.

Other uses of the sexual and reproductive body were as alarming to those wielding political and economic power. Slave women in the eighteenth-century Caribbean, the Belgian Congo, and other places where slavery and oppression prevailed, delved into their repertoire of bodily knowledge to prevent conception. They refused to give birth to more slaves and oppressed workers for imperialists and slave owners because of the horrendous conditions they knew their children would suffer. From the end of the nineteenth century down to the present day, women in those colonized countries or in the wealthy countries of the North also began what has been called a "birth control revolution," cutting the birth rate of Europe and the United States in half. Politicians such as Theodore Roosevelt of the United States accused them of carrying out a traitorous "birth strike" that would weaken the nation. In fact, although for many the reduction in fertility was based on the rising cost of raising children, there were some activists who saw birth control as a way of protesting the conditions of motherhood, including women's lack of rights over their children, their lower pay, bad medical and sanitary conditions, denial of access to divorce, and male violence in the family. The body has thus been a major force in women's politics.

Simultaneously, as feminists knew, governments have long regulated women's bodies and both male and female sexuality. Chinese theories of bodily harmony and the balance necessary for good health put a time limit on each sexual act performed by the emperor. His chief servant kept track of the time and then announced when it was over. Governments regularly monitored women's sexual activity, usually punishing them more severely than men for adultery and other sexual violations well into modern times. By awarding a woman's wages to her husband as his property, European and US governments essentially made women sexual servants with no rights to personal autonomy because they had no money to support themselves or their children. Simultaneously, marital rape was rarely acknowledged because a wife's body was seen as accessible to her husband at all times and under any circumstances. Governments often interpreted rape as a woman's fault, even mandating that she be killed if raped or allowing male relatives to do it without punishment. In many of these cases, killing women who had been raped was seen as preserving family honor. Even where rape was interpreted as a crime perpetrated by a man, convictions were extremely hard to obtain, right down to the present day. As part of Rich's intended meaning in her term "compulsory heterosexuality," it is not hard to see in these examples the force and compulsion applied to keep women's bodies behaving according to the rules of heterosexuality that privileged males and reinforced their power.

In many societies the use of birth control or even circulating knowledge of birth control has been legislated as a crime, meaning that governments have long been involved in women's sexuality, directly interfering in it. This was true in Nazi Germany for so-called Aryan women as well as for all women in the United States into the 1960s. Permission to use birth control, as we see in the case of Nazi Germany and the United States, has been denied to some groups—especially white women—and forced upon others. In the United States black women in particular were victims of forced sterilization, while in Nazi Germany Roma and Jewish women had access to birth control although they were not forced to use it. In the 1970s, India also instituted a policy of virtually forced sterilization to reduce population growth. District leaders there received bonuses for those women who would let themselves be sterilized, but the issue of compulsion was foremost: husbands would force their wives to be sterilized because they too might be compensated or receive political favors.

The rules and practices of embodiment have thus generally not operated to the benefit of women. Even basic medical research and health care continue to benefit men more than women. Thus, when the women's movement developed after World War II, activists were overwhelmingly concerned with women's rights to control their own bodies. For them, such control centered on the right to access birth control technology, which was rapidly evolving in the 1950s and 1960s. The birth control pill's development had been avidly pursued by Mexican and US researchers, and they succeeded in the 1950s in perfecting an effective one. Lobbying for access to birth control, those who achieved it came to feel the force of compulsory heterosexuality in regular campaigns to prevent its availability. Today those rights are under assault with the idea that "traditional" cultural values—that is, "compulsory heterosexuality" and all its ramifications—should not be disturbed.

Honor killings and horrific punishments meted out to victims of rape also outrage activists. Honor killings in which a woman is murdered because she wears Western clothing, is raped, or otherwise departs from conduct deemed appropriate by her family or society occur regularly around the world. Instances have taken place in the United States and Europe as well as in Asia and Africa. The idea behind honor killings is that women's behavior is not an individual matter but one where family reputation has been harmed or religious norms broken. It makes no difference whether the bodily conduct said to justify the killing is an action taken deliberately by the woman or whether it is the result of an attack by some other person. Sexual violence against a woman or girl, for example, justifies the killing of that woman or girl. The autonomy of the body remains an issue of heightened concern and debate in most cultures and in Women's Studies today.

Body politics also focus on the genital cutting of girls across Africa and to some extent in other parts of the world. Called genital mutilation by its opponents, the practice is denounced from a number of perspectives. The intense pain of the cutting is one objection, along with the risk of infection or sterilization. Others oppose the practice for powerful and more abstract reasons by calling attention to the lack of consent and bodily autonomy in the act. Because adults—both male and female—generally subject young girls to genital cutting or back the procedure indirectly, there is hardly room for resistance or the ability for young girls to articulate their opposition. Critics point additionally to the economic support of the cutting by those practitioners who perform it—mostly women—because they are paid for their work. It is a well-defined job that brings a fee and is thus defended as a livelihood. Reformers counter this with the suggestion for greater job creation where genital cutting is the norm, as a way of providing alternative jobs. A final objection to the practice of genital cutting is its effect not only psychologically but physically on girls whose sexuality becomes attenuated because of removal of the clitoris in particular.

However, the diminution of sexual desire is one reason behind genital cutting: the girl's sexual desire is reduced in preparation for a deep relationship with her husband, not the superficial one of sexual stimulation. Moreover, this potential husband is led to expect a bride who has been made clean by the removal of a large part of her genitalia and so families shy away from making their daughters less desirable as brides. Finally, supporters point to the lifelong camaraderie built among girls of the same age who experience genital cutting as a group ritual and whose evolving life course as a woman depends on the ties and solidarity based on this rite of passage.

THE BODY POLITICS OF DISABILITY

Body politics in Women's Studies also and importantly have come to include an analysis of the place of those who are not fully able-bodied based on social, physical, and cultural norms. The disability of people encompasses a wide range of physical and mental conditions including those who experience blindness, deafness, or a different capacity of the limbs or other body parts than those with normate bodies. Cerebral palsy, Down's syndrome, and post-polio syndrome affect many, while disability can also include mental and physical challenges that may go unnoticed such as multiple sclerosis (MS), chronic fatigue syndrome, and many other conditions that are called "invisible" disabilities. The range of disabilities is vast, and researchers note that across the lifespan at least 90 percent of humans will experience disability, whether temporary or permanent, including pregnancy and old age.

Disability has become a Women's Studies field of investigation because of its connections to the body, the prominent discrimination heaped on those who are not able-bodied, and the role of gender in the experience of disability. The pioneer activist and scholar Rosemarie Garland-Thomson pointed to the ways in which disability is used in fiction to indicate villains or people lacking in moral uprightness. Pathetic characters are often the disabled as well—Tiny Tim in Charles Dickens' *A Christmas Carol*, for example. US "celebrity chef" Gabrielle Hamilton's *New York Times* article about running a kitchen featured a blind chef as her example of all that was abhorrent in the world of cuisine. The account of his blindness showed an author full of disgust for the disabled and said a great deal about the newspaper's own attitudes toward disability. Men have expressed a similar disgust with women's bodies and disability researchers point to the same lesser value and intelligence attributed to both the disabled and women. They both serve as the "other" to the able-bodied and male. Films especially focus on any deviations from the bodily norm, and the public in general can often only see disability, not humanity. As one Disability Studies scholar noted, "People don't want to talk with me about music or good books but rather to ask how I'm coping with my [disability] misery."

Beyond general discrimination towards those with disabled bodies is the more focused issue of women and disability. For one thing, pregnant women are seen to be crippled both mentally and physically because of their condition, and indeed this can carry over into the evaluation of all women. Pregnancy, although eulogized, has yet to be fully analyzed from an intersectional approach that factors in both Disability Studies and Women's Studies. The extreme cultural emphasis on women's physical beauty can also cause those who deviate from those norms to be considered inferior and less worthy. Physical space is generally designed for the able-bodied, but because women are more likely to have household responsibilities, problems with design for normate bodies can affect them more. Whereas many Women's Studies students and teachers may see abortion as part of women's rights, some disability activists call it the genocide of the disabled. In other words, the majority of abortions in the West are performed to eliminate fetuses with disabilities, while those outside the West are used to abort girls—again constituting a link between gender and disability. Moreover, among women there are many varieties of disability that can affect them by race and class. These call for varying activist and analytical positions. Thus, disability among women calls for a return to intersectionality, taking into account where gender, race, and class work together to the great disadvantage of disabled women. Solutions to issues involving gender and disability demand an intersectional approach.

Gender works actively among disabled people in other ways. Men with post-polio syndrome find that their masculinity is once again at risk, as they are unable to "be a man" once the syndrome strikes them in their later years. Activists have noted that the disability movement itself is highly gendered, with men claiming leadership positions in disability groups. This has resulted in greater attention being devoted to those disabilities that affect men. Additionally, because men as a group have more funds for their care, disabled women may suffer as a result of gender hierarchy at work in the economy.

The definition and analysis of disability depend as much on location as other Women's Studies issues do. In Africa, for instance, the most serious disability for women is infertility. Children afford status but they are also part of the definition of able-bodiedness. Definitions of wellness revolve around women's reproductive health, menaced over the last century by colonialism, which left many too malnourished to reproduce. Additionally the many civil wars in Africa and police violence under apartheid have left women disabled. Some forms of disability are seen as holy in certain cultures; other forms as monstrous and demonic, depending on the region. Disabled women in the Middle East receive less assistance because of gender segregation and women's lower degree of participation in the formal workforce. In countries where gender segregation is common, disabled men and their concerns dominate political activism.

In the past, people born with characteristics of both sexes were called hermaphrodites while in our time they are labeled intersexed. These people too are important to Women's Studies research and understanding. In the older view the hermaphrodite was both fully male and fully female, but today we know that there are several dozen ways in which chromosomes, sexual organs, secondary sex characteristics, and hormones may occur blended in humans. These individuals with blended sexual characteristics challenge the clear-cut boundaries of heterosexual difference. To restore the individual to an identity of either male or female, doctors perform surgery to "fix" these bodies to conform to social expectations and beliefs—that is, the belief that there are only two sexes. In many cases such operations have caused a lifetime of pain, leading to today's activism to leave the intersexed alone.

The goal of maintaining heterosexuality is clear in the case of medical intervention on the bodies of the intersexed. Doctors, along with society at large, apparently feel that the intersexed will bring disorder to the entire gender order that is based so powerfully on the two-sex model. Some doctors believe that homosexuality will increase if the intersexed are not "fixed" because, being of two sexes, they will inevitably be having a sexual relationship with someone of their own sex. Most of those intersexed whose bodies have been made to conform to the heterosexual model express in surveys their distress at being sexually less complex and in fact "streamlined." Those who have been left with their original bodies are generally content. For Women's Studies, the intersexed are important in understanding the expanding struggle for human rights, sexual diversity, and the transformation of social values.

DEBATING, DEFINING, AND DESIGNING EMBODIMENT

Women's Studies has taken up the issue of embodiment, focusing in particular on both society's role in producing normative bodies and individual practices of embodiment. One tack has been to see the cultural forces that determine women's body images and as a result create sexual difference and identity. These forces include first and foremost the media, which since World War II has projected the most desirable woman as thin, young, beautiful, and often light in skin color. This desirable body is then deployed to sell products, be they alcohol and automobiles, shaving products and soap, or various services such as plastic surgery. Studying the body as a cultural production and as a purveyor of commodities is an important activity in Women's Studies because such cultural visions exercise power over women.

Yet there is a range of reactions to the commodification and glamorizing of women's bodies. Women and girls have responded positively, taking glamour as a norm to be followed even to the extent of having their bodies reshaped and enhanced surgically. Many women and girls have multiple procedures over the course of a lifetime and choose such procedures as a form of agency. The emphasis on the beautiful female face and body was criticized by some feminists in the 1960s when they crowned a sheep Miss America and tossed their confining undergarments in the trash. The objection to beauty pageants was not only that they set an unrealistic and superficial standard of female beauty but that they focused almost exclusively on physical characteristics. Women, the implication was, had little to offer except their physical attractions. Today, however, some feminist scholars outside the West interpret beauty pageants as liberating in that they emphasize women's autonomy. These displays break codes of women's modesty and seclusion by bringing the body into the public spotlight in such countries as India and post-Soviet Russia.

At another end of the spectrum, large women have defended oversized bodies, finding in them signs of power and freedom from cultural constraints, even from cultural imprisonment in the image of the hyper-thin woman. There are singing groups and comedy groups of hefty women—most of them mocking, flaunting, or defending their size. At still another extreme are those who suffer from eating disorders including bulimia and anorexia—both of these efforts to control the body's size, especially making it very thin. These eating disorders have come to surpass hysteria as problematic diseases of the body for women. Whereas hysteria—once the dominant affliction affecting women a century ago—has virtually disappeared, cases of anorexia have soared. The most severe cases lead to death, including those of a famed Brazilian model, Ana Carolina Reston, and media celebrities such as Karen Carpenter. Analysts have seen in cases of individuals withholding the nourishment they need or vomiting after meals an endeavor to assert autonomy—which women often don't fully possess despite the centrality of autonomy to the possession of full citizenship in the modern nation state. Others interpret anorexia and bulimia as ways of preventing the development of adult female sexual characteristics over which men would take control by keeping the body childlike in its appearance. Still others see in anorexia an abject condition in which the anorexic separates herself from normal society and appears outside of and even repugnant to the world of human interactions—again a form of agency, however troubling. Finally, there is a new emphasis on the anorexic as a controller of their destiny, a subject who experiences, changes, tries to interact, has values of her own—that is, a constructed individual whose being flows and often attempts to achieve a healthy personhood. This being is far removed from the subject whom earlier feminist theorists believed they could pin down to an identifiable patient, whose body was clearly ill.

At this point the cultural representation of the body intersects with its physicality. This is the body that most would call the "real" body. Often this body is seen as straightforward and a solid biological entity composed of indisputable facts such as visible sexual characteristics and the experiences of illness, maturation, aging, pain, and death. As the physical body intersects with culture we see both medical inequalities in the treatment of women's illnesses and in the violence done to the female body that is undernourished, beaten, or even murdered on the basis of the lower value that cultures place on women. The aspects of embodiment that interest us most as we move ahead are the body's sexual differences, pleasures, and behaviors that we gather under the term sexuality. Like the "real" body, the body's sexuality is usually seen as fairly straightforward—straight, gay, lesbian, or bisexual. Women's Studies research has complicated these easy definitions.

COMPULSORY HETEROSEXUALITY AND THE LESBIAN EXPERIENCE

Adrienne Rich's essay on "Compulsory Heterosexuality" was celebrated in the West when it first appeared in 1980. Rich pointed to the idea that heterosexuality was a believed in and fully accepted norm and that this norm was forced on women by men. Violence, laws, and the invocation of "traditional values" all served to give men sexual access to women on men's terms and to disempower them economically and politically. Women could and do act as the enforcers as well because they accept that men are superior in intelligence and overall worth. Most importantly, in devaluing women's desires and achievements and thereby enforcing a relationship with the more highly valued male, compulsory heterosexuality prevented women from relating to one another as women. As a result compulsory heterosexuality impeded and devalued the "lesbian experience."

For Rich, the lesbian experience was not only about sexuality but about a range of beneficial relationships that women could have with one another without men. They would then become "women-identified women," that is women who could appreciate womanhood instead of taking men as the norm for all that was worthwhile in society. The power of Rich's essay was such that Women's Studies made lesbian experience a major part of the curriculum, studying lesbian essays, poetry, and fiction that both preceded and followed it and opening up a fuller study of sexuality and sexual identity. Distinguishing themselves from gay men at times because of their different experience, lesbian scholars and scholars of lesbianism have ranged widely to cover the various aspects of this experience, and many break with Rich in emphasizing or focusing on same-sex desire and practice. They often defend pornography, whereas many straight feminists don't, because it promotes desire and erotic fantasies. For many straight women, it is a form of violence against women, whereas for many lesbians accepting pornography is to accept their sexual desire in all its possible forms of expression.

Studying lesbian sexuality and sexual identity is crucial to breaking down categories and challenging stereotypes of lesbian behaviors such as "butch–femme" norms in relationships. Much of the time ignored, the complexities of lesbian identity have shown it to be as broad a phenomenon as can be imagined. It does not merely mirror heterosexuality in butch–femme relationships, in which one partner adopts a quasi-male role and the other a quasi-female one. Nor is it mostly platonic, as suggested by Rich and others. Instead, lesbian practices are rich and multiple. Sexual radicals among lesbians wear leather, pierce their bodies, and practice sado-masochism—all of these ingredients of their relationship that break down any number of stereotypes. Indeed, sado-masochism has been defended and even celebrated as a form of equality, as partners change from being the dominant individual to being the submissive one with regularity. Simultaneously other lesbians assert their reproductive needs by having children and raising them in lesbian families. In some parts of the world lesbians and gays lobby for gay marriage, again challenging stereotypes and norms. Among these norms is an earlier one of the "committed bachelor" and the spinster housemates. Women's Studies brings the content and development of these relationships into the classroom so that the full range of sexual identity, experience, and activism can be understood.

NATURE SPEAKS ABOUT SEX

For a very long time, the world of nature has been taken by scientists to be a model of heterosexuality. Any time change is proposed among the sexes in human societies, critics point to the example of nature, where everything is clearly divided into male and female and where heterosexual monogamy and the family are said to rule. Women's Studies and other research on the natural world have come up with new findings. For one thing, scientists some three hundred years ago described the reproduction of plants in terms of male and female copulation, emphasizing the sexual frenzy they experienced as their orgasms produced new blossoms and seeds. Pistils and stamens were designated male and female, and the entire heterosexual schema assigned to plants became a model for the assumed naturalness of heterosexuality in humans and for male–female complementarity. Even the classification "mammals" came about because of a fascination with the female breast, leading to a false naming of entire species. That is, some animals with the classification "mammals" do not have mammae.

The situation was little different in descriptions of reproduction in the animal kingdom. Scientists have until recently described all animal sexuality as heterosexual and "practical" in its end goal of reproduction. Moreover, scientific studies went on to show that this sexuality was a form of monogamous heterosexuality even in cases where animals appeared to be having a variety of sexual relationships. The heterosexual model of gender dimorphism ruled in the scientific world as well as in the social and political world. If all animals were heterosexual and monogamous, that should be the way of humans. Monogamy and heterosexuality were "natural" and, as such, should be adopted by everyone.

Since the beginning, Women's Studies research has shown the heterosexual model of reproduction and sexuality supposedly found in nature to be a fantasy of earlier scientists—and one that has been perpetrated as scientific fact. Not only do we have the demonstrated facts of the existence of multiple sexes in humans, as shown earlier in this chapter, but we also have many examples of multiple sexualities in the animal kingdom. Some animal species, for example, have only females and nonetheless reproduce—a species of lizards provide just one example of such reproduction. Scientists now admit to there being a wide variety of sexual behavior and reproduction among animals. For example, animals have group sex, pleasurable same-sex relationships where no reproduction is involved, same-sex reproduction as in the case of the lizards, and in fact an entire spectrum of sexual practices. In the animal kingdom sexuality is not necessarily attached to reproduction, nor is reproduction uniformly heterosexual. According to scientific findings, nature is no longer exclusively binary and heterosexual. It is less grimly regular, showing, as one researcher puts it, a wide range of natural "exuberance."

QUEER ACTS CHALLENGE ALL SEXUAL IDENTITIES

Another challenge to clear-cut and binary definitions of sexual identity, both heterosexual and homosexual, began to take shape decades ago and was slow to evolve into queer activism and beliefs. In June 1969 in the Greenwich Village neighborhood of New York, police raided a bar that gay men were known to frequent. Some would be taken away and booked, others would be shaken down for money. Generally homosexuals caught up in the police dragnet would be harassed as a matter of course. The police tactics worked because, despite an active gay scene, homosexuals in the 1950s and 1960s kept a low profile as part of their drive to gain the decriminalization of their relationships. They also kept their sexuality "closeted" as a way of earning a living or keeping good jobs, given their criminalization in law and the relentless discrimination against them. The reaction at Stonewall that night in June changed all that because suddenly the patrons of the bar and of other bars fought back, rioting across the Stonewall area, and finally declaring that they would no longer tolerate police harassment. They came out of the closet, as the expression went, and instead asserted their identity as gay. Gay pride followed, replacing silence, and ever since then the end of June has seen gay pride parades taking place around the world in commemoration of the world-changing events at Stonewall.

The AIDS crisis that struck the gay community in the 1980s and that continues to afflict millions around the world brought lesbians and gays to ally with one another after disagreements over male domination of activism on behalf of homosexual rights. Lesbians, like their male counterparts and straight feminists, watched in alarm as their friends and acquaintances were struck down by the AIDS virus. No help was in sight, leading to the creation of groups such as ACT-UP, an organization in the United States that confronted the public by staging loud demonstrations to obtain funding for AIDS research, education, and relief. ACT-UP was loud, defiant, and unashamed, as its members refused to hide the devastation caused by AIDS. Such groups took shape around the world, sometimes being led by unions, as in South Africa, but generally with an active gay membership.

From ACT-UP and like-minded groups came the defiant self-naming of similarly defiant individuals as "queer." Refusing to behave quietly about their sexuality, they first launched the term as an extension of the rebellion that had begun with Stonewall. In adopting the defiant stance of ACT-UP queers went beyond celebrating gay pride by converting a word that stigmatized those in same-sex relationships or with same-sex and other sexual identities into a word that would harass, shock, shame, and otherwise assault homophobic society. It began as an assault on straightness and aimed for a separation from straight society, but there was more to come.

"Queer" is now a broad way of looking at the world, as we have learned in the preceding chapter. Yet queer theory has come to challenge the study of sexuality in Women's Studies, which was founded on the model of male–female difference and often on male–female antagonisms. Although Women's Studies is continually changing, its views were initially binary, although increasingly the functioning of male–female binaries is called into question—for example in the explosion of the belief that there are only two sexes.

Queer theory further disturbed Women's Studies and Gender Studies categories when it ultimately dismissed the idea of binaries or categories entirely. It sees none at all in its most extreme form because queer theory runs parallel to the new findings of biological science and the practice of trans people (for example) to the extent that "sex" is a pliable category. It accepts the corollary of post-modernism that gender and sexuality are not so capable of being pinned down to definable categories. It also transforms some of the foundational investigations of Women's Studies scholars into family, kinship, and sexual practices because its takes few of these as fundamental.

One of queer theory's first attacks was on definitions of gay, lesbian, trans, and bi as fixed in their opposition to heterosexuality. Queer theory did not begin by looking at the categories included in gay, lesbian, trans, and bi but rather it confronted heterosexuality. In attacking heterosexuality and heterosexual identity, queer theory investigates all societies for their homosexual prohibition. In this case, it was difficult to draw the line between heterosexuality and homosexuality because of the naturalness of same-sex attraction.

Animals, it was discovered, found companionship—apart from sexuality—and on the basis of that companionship raised offspring that were biologically not necessarily their own. Queers pointed to the practices of the past 30 years where non-related couples have raised families that were not the result of their own sexual coupling. They also developed communities that had nothing to do with either kinship or sexual identity. In other words, queers and queer theory pointed to their distinction from both normative hetero-sexual couples/families and the traditional homosexual rejection of reproductive sex by sometimes embracing reproduction for them-selves and sometimes not or even by raising unrelated children.

In sum, queers may be seen as breaking barriers, boundaries, and normative causes—be they straight or homosexual—even those of feminism, gay pride, or any other kind of identity politics. If queer activists often do support such causes as a matter of allying themselves politically to achieve an end, their main work aims at eliminating the need for such activism by causing people to rethink identities to the point of eliminating fixed categories. Queer theory in fact joins feminist theory in questioning the category "woman" as it has been defined over the centuries.

CONCLUSION

Over the decades, Women's Studies research has covered a great deal of ground when it comes to investigating sexual identity, behaviors, and beliefs. It began by looking at the repression of heterosexual women's sexuality in such Freudian theories as the one stating that a woman could only have a "mature" sexual relationship if she had a vaginal orgasm. It investigated claims that women's "hysteria"—a common condition of mental illness or eccentric behavior attributed to them—was rooted in sexual dysfunction. The enemies in these early studies of women's sexuality were, because of the belief in the male–female sexual binary, male doctors, psychologists, social workers, and other rule-enforcing personnel. The activism of lesbian feminists and then the work of scholars interested in lesbian sexuality have shifted attitudes in Women's Studies research to embrace more complicated views of women's bodies and their sexuality.

Sexual norms and values vary around the world, with some holding the intersexed, for example, in high regard, and others trying to fix those whose bodies do not conform to the two-sex model in order to keep society molded by heterosexuality and the two-sex model. Most societies alter the body in some way, through procedures on the skin and torso and even on the genitals. The complexity of attitudes towards embodiment finds its full range in Women's Studies research, although in many parts of the world attention paid to the body in classrooms varies considerably. Some want attention focused on issues of forced abortion, the continuation of forms of sexual slavery, honor killings, and sexual selection, while for others the multiple forms of sexual identity and sexual expression are at the top of the list of classroom work. Queer theory would eradicate the study of sexual identity and difference by denying the existence of any such distinctions and forms. In some ways queer theory works to validate those who think that sexuality is not important and that in fact capitalism and the global exploitation of people are far more urgent topics for investigation and discussion. At present, understandings of embodiment, sexuality, and sexual identity are more complex than ever before, thanks in large part to the work of Women's Studies.

SUGGESTED READING

Brier, Jennifer (2009) *Infectious Ideas: U.S. Political Response to the AIDS Crisis*. Chapel Hill, NC: University of North Carolina Press.

Butler, Judith (1993) *Bodies that Matter: On the Discursive Limits of "Sex."* New York: Routledge.

Fryer, David (2010) *Thinking Queerly: Race, Sex, Gender, and the Ethics of Identity*. Boulder, CO: Paradigm Press, 2010.

Garland-Thomson, Rosemarie (1997) *Extraordinary Bodies: Figuring Physical Disability in American Culture and Literature*. New York: Columbia University Press.

Hutchison, Beth and Smith, Bonnie G. (eds.) (2004) *Gendering Disability*. New Brunswick: Rutgers University Press.

Journal of the History of Sexuality (1990 to the present).

Kang, Miliann (2010) *The Managed Hand: Race, Gender, and the Body in Beauty Service Work*. Berkeley, CA: University of California Press.

Livingston, Julie (2005) *Debility and Moral Imagination in Botswana*. Bloomington, IN: Indiana University Press.

Matera, Mark, Bastian, Misty L. and Kingsley Kent, Susan (2011) *The Women's War of 1929: Gender and Violence in Colonial Nigeria*. New York: Macmillan Palgrave.

Puar, Jaspir (2007) *Terrorist Assemblages: Homonationalism in Queer Times*. Durham: Duke University Press.

Warin, Megan (2010) *Abject Relations: Everyday Worlds of Anorexia*. New Brunswick, NJ: Rutgers University Press.

8

CLASSROOMS, CONTROVERSIES, AND CITIZENSHIP

Women's Studies aimed to change the classroom and believed it would change the university—often as a prelude to changing the world through knowledge. In this chapter we look at the classroom, its practices, and their relationship to citizenship. What was the thinking behind both the assertion that change is and was needed in the world at large and that Women's Studies was the program that would bring about such change? We want to consider some of the goals of citizenship for women and the ways in which Women's Studies pedagogy and classroom practices are central to the cause of women's citizenship. Finally. this chapter points to contentious issues in Women's Studies classrooms and tries to look at them from different angles. The objective in this part of the chapter is to subject our fervently held beliefs to a variety of challenges and to build critical skills that can be used when faced with difficult issues both in the university and in public life. Women's Studies, it is often believed, is an exercise in developing civic skills, whether for the classroom community or the broader one.

In this chapter we also consider whether Women's Studies should reflect feminist politics both explicitly and implicitly. From the beginning, as we have seen, feminism was connected to Women's Studies. Feminism sparked the commitment to do research on women, and in the early years there was hardly a scholar of women who wasn't a feminist. Some increasingly saw problems with this situation given that knowledge under the scientific method was supposed to be above politics. If one were going to be a scholar, could one be politically committed to feminism at the same time? Even more daunting was the question of whether one could actively advocate on behalf of women in the classroom or in the university and still uphold standards of impartiality. This was especially pressing, as we have seen, because members of the university community charged Women's Studies with not being a group of impartial scholars but with being political before being scholarly. As we have seen in our consideration of feminist methodology, there are other solutions.

That is, different locations will produce different questions and different answers to the questions of feminism, pedagogy, and citizenship and these differences will produce contentious classrooms. Some will be happy with explicit feminist strivings for equality. Others will aim for solidarity with men and take that as their main concern in the classroom. Still others will explicitly reject all that is Western, especially the clear-cut aspirational goal to be valued as equal when the deck is stacked against people of non-male gender, non-white race, the impoverished, those with a non-normate body, and those of different sexualities. There will be some who will for these reasons believe feminism to be less than helpful. We believe that the classroom is one place to articulate both rejections and optimism. The feminist classroom should lead to thoughtfulness and reflection and if possible dismantle some of the "controlling images" that segment us by race, ethnicity, class, religion, and gender.

Another difficult question is whether Women's Studies has to be "relevant." That is, does Women's Studies have an obligation to address current social and political problems facing women or can it look on women's lives more broadly? For example, can Women's Studies look at women authors of fiction from the nineteenth century even though they may not address today's issues? People debate whether Women's Studies professors need to shape the curriculum to be contemporary in outlook instead of examining women's writing for the sheer beauty it might offer. Could one simply admire women's paintings or sculpture as works of art, or do sexual politics need to be the most important consideration in studying artistic creations? Couldn't we simply investigate with the goal of finding a bias-free truth distinct from politics?

Finally, the question arises of whether teachers needed to create a feminist classroom based on the values of the feminist movement. One tenet of feminism is that women should be appreciated for their talents in the same way that men have been valued. Other values of feminism have been leaderlessness—that is, a non-hierarchical approach to social groups and an explicit acknowledgment of the power dynamics that might be at work in the classroom. But because feminism is now open to question, especially given the multiple sites of power and disempowerment, there are many vantage points from which different kinds of knowledge can radiate. The idea was also to have feminist processes in the classroom whereby the sharing of ideas would prevail over the kind of slashing critique of others' ideas that often characterized the male ideal, but perhaps that is passé. It may be that more not less critique is necessary. The class will discuss processes to be used in critical discussion as much as it considers the content of those discussions.

WOMEN AND CITIZENSHIP

The rights of citizenship are important in our modern world, and Women's Studies scholars around the world examine the nature of women's citizenship today. One motivating force in women's global activism is the accomplishment of the full and equal right to participate in public affairs and political life. Women in Asia, Africa, and Latin America have recently been at the forefront of understanding and developing citizens' rights. The challenges to women's citizenship are present almost everywhere in the form of legal restrictions on their participation, overwork that absorbs all their time and energy, and automatic assumptions about women's lower intelligence. Ruling elites in countries with a heritage of colonialism and business imperialism offer another serious impediment to women's participation in the life of the nation. Under colonialism, as we have seen, women faced forms of oppression not faced by men. In national liberation struggles the health of the nation was advanced as a reason for women not to press for their own well-being. Once independence came the same anti-colonial rhetoric was used to tell women that their rights needed to be delayed in the cause of nation-building. Gaining and practicing the rights of citizenship has been a challenge for women everywhere. Women need to gain a sense of belonging in their communities—local, national, and even the larger community that is developing around the world.

To gain the rights of citizenship, NGOs have sprung up in Africa and Latin America to stir women to advocate for their rights. Women at the grassroots have developed civic skills such as lobbying for clean water, sewage disposal, neighborhood safety, and women's literacy. All of these build both the skills needed for citizenship and advance citizenship itself. Such activism contrasts with some programs to advance women's citizenship in several countries of Africa. There "first ladies" are designated by their husbands to develop women's participation in public life. Such initiatives have ended up empowering elite women instead of empowering all women, because the upper classes are mostly involved in these projects. Such programs may have led to the start of Women's Studies programs or the development of groups of elite women to oversee the construction of housing, but it is not the same as the civic action of communities of women at the grassroots who create a sense of belonging in the face of the nation's policies of exclusion.

Developments that threaten women's full citizenship include structural adjustment programs, government sponsorship of sex tourism, and government participation in the militarization of the world. Because the latter stresses violent masculinity, women's rights in public are at risk, as are those of citizens more generally. Rape, whether during civil wars or as part of the daily dysfunctionality of supposedly safe communities like those in the United States, is particularly effective in dampening women's sense of welcome as equal citizens in a healthy nation of valued participants. Structural Adjustment Programs forced on developing governments in order for them to receive much-needed loans demand cutting national budgets, which often means cutting girls' and women's access to education, leaving them lacking many of the skills and the information needed for citizenship. Government sponsorship of sex tourism, based largely though not exclusively on the sex work of women, speaks volumes about the very low levels of respect in which women are held by community leaders. Is developing a sense of civic belonging so central to citizenship possible under the conditions that exist around the world?

A CHILLY CLIMATE IN THE CLASSROOM

For *Women's Studies: The Basics*, we draw an analogy between citizenship in the nation and citizenship in the classroom. The classroom is often said to be the training ground for citizenship. An undemocratic classroom, unlike an undemocratic state, is usually not good for women. If women do not fully and equally belong to the classroom, how can we consider that they belong to the larger communities in which they live? We take it for granted that in education teachers see their pupils as equally important in the process of learning and that students are valued no matter what their gender, race, or religion. The fundamental principle we adhere to is that everyone's ideas are treated equally just as a physician is assumed to treat all his or her patients equally. Studies undertaken long ago and more recently prove that such ideals are not put into practice.

The classroom is a chilly place for those who are not white, male, and straight. Those qualities determine who is recognized by teachers, whose answers meet with the most approval and elicit the most feedback, and who receives the best grade. Some of the first testing in the early days of the feminist movement involved giving evaluators such as teachers the same essay with women's and men's names attached alternately to the essays. Overwhelmingly, the same essay would be graded higher for a male name than a female name, suggesting that "scientific" or even fair standards were not used. Instead, evaluation was done on the basis of whether the author or test-taker was male or female. Social norms holding men in higher esteem formed the basis of evaluation rather than rational, professional, or neutral standards.

Another place where neutral observers found the classroom to be bad for women was in classroom discussions where class participation was taking place. The first study of gendered treatment of students—"The Classroom: A Chilly Climate for Women"—was sponsored by the Carnegie Foundation and published by the American Association of Colleges in 1982. Since then, studies have considered the inequitable treatment of racial, sexual, and other minorities and the impact such treatment has on their performance. The results do not look good for the educational situation of those who aren't white males in the West.

University teachers regularly asked women students for factual information while they asked their male students to explain what those facts meant and to give their thoughts about events. They regularly called on their male students while often ignoring the women. When women started to respond, the teacher would more often interrupt a woman's answer than that teacher would cut off a man. Male students received more feedback, with teachers interacting positively with their male students more often than they would with women. Overall, men were encouraged to speak and their speaking was more highly valued than women's participation was.

A particularly surprising finding of this study was that female as well as male teachers valued their male students more than they valued female students. However, we should not be surprised that women teachers follow the same norms as men do. It is shocking to some that women bosses treat women workers beneath them in status with the same disregard and even abuse as men treat those same women. If the social norm is not to value women, why wouldn't it be natural for women to hold to those same agreed-upon norms? So, even though I myself had to question my behavior as a teacher, in the long run, it was not surprising to have to do so. I, like most people, belong to a social order and to a community of commonly shared values. Although many teachers and students are now painfully aware of the tendency for women and other minority students to be sanctioned more than men and less favored, we must always be on the lookout as human beings to check for our own sexism, racism, classism, and other discriminatory behaviors.

Another aspect of the university involves not only emotional but possible physical harm. We now know that young students—both male and female—are subject to sexual predators in schools, where they are often silenced instead of reporting their abuse—a situation that appears to have existed for centuries. Even in universities young women are seen as prey by their teachers and graduate students. It is not uncommon for teachers to subject women students—supposedly people to be nurtured as young future citizens whose lives are to be expanded in terms of knowledge and character—to sexual harassment and even to rape. It may be suggested that good grades will follow sexual intercourse or that better letters of recommendation depend on sexual favors. Although colleges and universities around the world have constructed codes of conduct forbidding such activities, they are hardly followed. University teachers who rape students—a legal crime—are usually dealt with by the administration and the crimes never reported to the authorities. Offending teachers are bought off, while the women are made to sign away their rights to go to the police in exchange for getting their degrees. Women students know that their careers would be ruined should they protest such conditions or, in many cases, if they even reported an offender to the school administration.

Harm from the chilly climate is now well known and as teachers and students we must make the classroom a welcoming place so as not to harm those we teach and those with whom we study. Those who are interrupted or demeaned during discussions, graded on the basis of sexist or racist bias, or sexually pursued are disempowered as learners. We don't actually know if they are less capable because according to all studies they are graded as less capable. We also know from studies that the sexist and racist behavior of those in authority generally undermines student victims for life. They will drop out of school, or graduate with far less self-confidence, and behave as if they are less capable. Moreover, the validation given to less worthy men simply because they are men also leads to unfair claims throughout men's lives and creates a less fair social order. Given that the sum result of sexism, racism, homophobia, and other kinds of harmful behavior in the classroom is so negative, we need to make our classrooms fairer and more just through a consideration of best practice.

CONSCIOUSNESS-RAISING

One practice that can help in creating that fairness has been called "consciousness-raising." The idea of consciousness-raising involves talking about the issues involved in being a woman and coming to an awareness of the many ways in which males are privileged. This technique arose with the very beginnings of the women's movement in the 1960s when very few women in the West would have thought that they were discriminated against. Consciousness-raising groups sprang up, during which slowly and ever so cautiously participants would give voice to wrongs in the society, the workplace, in the home, and in personal relationships. In those days consciousness-raising moved at a glacial pace in many cases. People started with their own situations, for example, too much housework, and could hardly imagine that society as a whole discriminated against women. But as one consciousness-raising participant announced, there would come the "click" that suddenly gave a broad picture of women's lower status in the world, the workplace, and in the family.

Consciousness-raising also includes thinking about intersectionality—that is, as we saw in Chapter 3, the ways in which race, class, religion, sexuality, and ethnicity intersect with gender to add to inequality. It has become clear that one cannot think merely in terms of gender when involved in consciousness-raising. The focus on one category of human experience leaves too much out and distorts the full nature of discriminatory situations. As we have seen, focusing on women alone ignores the double discrimination faced by African-American women—as one example. To focus only on gender and race omits the category of sexuality, which may be added to the two other ingredients that make up life situations.

Class and race privilege and the normative status of the able-bodied are conditions that also become visible during consciousness-raising. It's not, for example, that students of color, or those living in poverty or the disabled don't see the privilege clearly. Rather, because white, able-bodied, and middle-class women see themselves as part of the norm, they are the ones who have only a partial view of the situation. Their class, race, and bodily privilege are not noticed and they focus on gender. Becoming aware of one's privileged position and then using that awareness in positive ways is another part of consciousness-raising. They need to figure out how to make alliances and to correct for their situation. Consciousness-raising deals with intersectionality—that is, the wide and overlapping range of privilege, discrimination, identity, and subordination. Consciousness-raising is difficult on many levels.

Reactions to a sudden awareness or a growing consciousness can be harsh. Because of the many attacks on feminism in the past decades, it is often hard to deal with such issues. There have been students for whom the "click" of recognition brought tears. "I can't believe that this has been going on for centuries and never changes," said one upset young woman in my Women's Studies class. Young and older women alike have to deal with the slurs against those who have a raised consciousness. They may be labeled bitches or men-haters or castrators or with any number of other names. Although a raised consciousness is a source of incredible strength, it is also difficult to sustain when social values say that women should not be empowered to defend themselves. The idea—long fought over the past decades—is that women should "suffer and be still." It is the condition that John Stuart Mill, coached by his wife Harriet Taylor Mill, noted more than a century ago when he wrote that women were supposed to be slaves to men, but willing and loving slaves.

Another problem with consciousness-raising in the classroom, especially when there may be no men present at all, is that men's privilege nonetheless fills the atmosphere. The idea is that male values are fixed in us and also in society more broadly so that sometimes women students may censor themselves when they say something that contradicts widely held opinions about women. Women who come to feel themselves suddenly empowered to speak may not go beyond simply speaking about their own condition if it means criticizing widely held beliefs. For example, they may speak about their own feeling of powerlessness but not want to confront the invisible power of masculinity because to do so goes against unspoken social norms. When I first taught a women's history class, students regularly deferred to the one or two men in the room, saying that they mostly wanted to hear male opinions. But men's opinions ring in students' ears even when there are no men present, and they can censor women's thought and speech even in their absence.

A reason for confusion and dismay in consciousness-raising is that there are two paradoxical beliefs in society that are held simultaneously. The first is that everyone is equal; the second is that men are better than women. Consciousness-raising in the classroom or anywhere else goes against the fundamental belief that women are equal to men. If women students note any inequality they have gone against the gendered social contract in which men bond in the name of equal citizenship and at the same time use their power together to perpetuate women's inequality. Thus, a consciousness-raised woman or one who identifies as feminist is often ridiculed, verbally abused, or even assaulted for daring to speak up for herself and against inequality because she is going against the idea that everyone is equal, when all the statistics show clearly that they are not.

So consciousness-raising has come to include not only participating in discussions but building the courage to give voice to situations of inequality and to name and analyze that condition.

Again, it is an exercise in dismantling the "controlling images" of women's second-classness so prevalent in almost every corner of the world. Because many are afraid to name this inequality, it is important to build community in the classroom (or anywhere else for that matter). In this way, approval for this kind of speaking and making the speaker feel that she is safe in speaking of social and personal wrongs create a sense of belonging. The classroom community must provide a caring atmosphere for all participants and one where students can deal with issues in the most open and insightful way possible. Like a citizen, one must feel a valued participant and one whose opinion is important to be heard.

CONTENTIOUS ISSUES IN THE CLASSROOM

Women's Studies classrooms are full of controversy, and how we manage our controversies productively demands all of our skill and concern for community values. Citizenship is about bringing forth our disagreements and different values; confronting differences and analyzing disagreements make up community life in a democracy. Differences spark creativity even as they may provoke anger; recognizing the combination as productive advances our discussion of contentious issues.

Today, surprisingly to some, a contentious issue is feminism. Young women find it associated with man-hating and shrillness. Feminists are unattractive in their complaints. In part some of these ideas come from media stereotypes—its diffusion of "controlling images"—and a lack of information about feminism's actual meaning and its goals. However, others not liking feminism or rejecting the term for themselves will see alternative modes of engagement as more important. Racial and ethnic beliefs also influence attitudes toward feminism. Students from different parts of the world, like Women's Studies faculty members themselves, will likewise differ about feminism, supporting womanism or post-feminism or queerness as preferable. There is much to learn from both small and large group discussions of feminism. It is important for knowledgeable participants to come up with accurate information about what feminism has or hasn't stood for and to assess shortcomings, mistakes, and different meanings of feminism depending on one's location.

Some reject feminism because of the variety of standpoints and theories they represent. Among the range of queer theorists, for example, it is not uncommon to espouse the erasing of all categories of difference and a refusal to work for the progressive and basically futile values that feminism represents in their eyes. They will propose new ways of thinking about the world, as we have seen. Many others contend that feminism is too Western or too centered on US theorists, researchers, organizations, and issues. Referencing women as prior to all categories, it will appear racist. Still others find feminism too negative and whiney, and definitely too outmoded. We believe that in a classroom as in democracy an atmosphere of belonging will produce the best results for airing sharply differing opinions and informed differences.

A second contentious issue in Women's Studies is religion, and this appears to be true in no matter what region of the world. In fact many controversies that seem to be unrelated do, on closer inspection, have a religious basis or connection. Religion itself is often seen as empowering by some and disempowering to women by others. For example, throughout time women have made sacred journeys for strength, healing, and to come into closer contact with the divine. Religious faith has provided a sense of spiritual well-being and a source of emotional comfort in times of stress. Even women outside of any creed find images of ancient goddesses and religious martyrs—Hindu, Greek, or Christian—inspiring. For many religion connects the living and the dead, buttressing traditions and giving a sense of wholeness in a fragmented world. It would be hard to overstate the importance of religion to many of the world's peoples, including the world's women.

Advocates for religion also find religious teachings full of admirable values. For example, admirers of Hinduism note that Hindu texts advocate oneness with nature and a sensitivity to the well-being of all the earth's creatures. Practitioners like Gandhi held that in Hindu belief there was neither caste nor gender nor race but only oneness with the cosmos. Religious texts also endorse virtues that protect—such as the idea of ahimsa, that is, to do no harm. In Christian texts the poor are valued above the rich, making upper-class pride and exclusiveness anti-Christian. A camel will pass through the eye of a needle, the biblical maxim goes, sooner than a rich man will get into heaven. The ill and suffering deserve compassion, while the poor should receive the wherewithal to live in dignity, virtually all religions teach us.

Others in Women's Studies classrooms find religion to be especially oppressive to women and to society as a whole, and the list of charges against religion is long. Primary among these charges is that the world's religions are for the most part controlled by men and that they are often used as a means of patriarchal domination of women in particular and of society generally. Additionally the control of religious institutions enriches those who dominate them in the present as in the past. Religion is often seen as opposing some of the scientific developments that women find important to their own and their children's well-being: contraception, vaccinations. Religion is thus seen as the opposite of secular progress, in which many students believe.

Women's Studies classrooms thus often focus on the harm done to women in the name of religion. For example, in many parts of the world there is heated discussion of veiling, with Women's Studies students feeling strongly on both sides of the issue. However, works such as Joan Scott's *Politics of the Veil* reveal a variety of reasons for women to adopt the headscarf, including rebellion against parents, a feeling of stylishness, religious commitment, social pressure, and so on. Classroom discussions allow this variety to come forth and be fully aired. Additionally, the fantasies of those who would forbid the veil, as in the French case, are often revealing to students. Furthermore, increased knowledge allows us all to see that lines are not always so clearly drawn among religious and secular women as asserted. In Morocco, for example, secular feminists and religious women interact and react. They borrow one another's tactics and platforms; the result is a form of hybridity. The discussion of religion as a polarizing system is one that can galvanize class discussion and simultaneously create community, if not consensus.

Other classrooms debate practices such as genital cutting (as described in Chapter 7) or others such as sati—the practice of a widow, young or old, a mother or childless, immolating herself on her husband's funeral pyre—or child marriage, in terms of both objections and endorsements. Endorsers will accredit the sati with great spirituality in her commitment to follow her husband in death and to be purified in reuniting with him. She has manifested devotion and even goddess-like qualities, performing miracles in some cases. However, those opposed to sati see such women as murdered by in-laws who find her a burden and want her funds. Politicians and community leaders likewise approve of sati if the act can be turned into a spectacle for them to lead and profit from. Thus anti-sati activists strip sati of its religious justification to interpret it as a strictly secular act against women often motivated by the rising consumerism (as are dowry deaths) in areas where it is practiced. The same is true of child marriage, which can also have religious endorsements as well as financial motivations.

From the beginning of Women's Studies the activism of students and teachers was still another subject of debate, simultaneously motivating discussion and silencing others. In the early days, activism was a motivating factor for the introduction of scholarship on women, and students and teachers alike were involved in promoting equality in the economy, reproductive rights, better jobs, and political power. Engagement with the campaign for sexual rights and with the struggle to address the AIDS crisis of the 1980s was also common. It was often Women's Studies students who prompted "Take Back the Night" marches and demonstrations for other feminist causes. They demanded that courses prepare them for the activism that they saw as their duty.

However, feminist activism bothers others in Women's Studies who want to see themselves as researchers. They do not want to be associated with the Western values and racial domination that feminism implies. Thus activism has prompted the charge that Women's Studies is Western and political and not scholarly—a charge that exists to this day. Is teaching activism, as some scholars contended, and are activists "better" than those simply studying the condition of women? While involved in these debates, some Women's Studies programs expanded to address the needs of women in prisons, non-traditional students, and distance learners as part of activism. They reached out to leaders in the hope of bringing greater attention to scholarly findings outside the academy. Whether the Women's Studies classroom and its outreach is or should be different from those in other subjects is a topic with many pros and cons and has been so since the beginning of the field. Does activism detract from objectivity or is objectivity always combined with a politics and interests—implicit or explicit? Is activism part of the Western "civilizing mission"? These topics make us aware of still further basic differences among students and teachers and among those in different parts of the world.

The advantages of feminist classrooms are that they allow us to work with the insights about education and society that conscious-ness-raising has provided and that they help empower students of all genders, races, classes, sexualities, and bodily types. That is, because it strives for equality and a voice for the voiceless a feminist class-room is more capable of empowering and broadening students' minds than one that harks back to traditional norms of discrimination and privilege. In fact, many would see a feminist classroom as the only just classroom because it consciously works to root out distortion of facts based on gender, race, and other inequities. Hierarchy is questioned. In short, a feminist classroom is one that actually embodies the rational, scientific, and democratic values to which most humans aspire. Those who see feminism as part of white domination, however, disagree.

Feminist practice often involved an investigation of hierarchy and a determination to abolish authority based on unjust claims. There was a sense that there should be leaderlessness among feminist groups; Western women did not uniformly apply this belief when dealing with women from the global South. Because women have dealt with so many oppressive forms of power and because they have also dealt with unjust authorities, an equalizing trend or hope should come as no surprise. Feminist classrooms often examine claims to authority and power not only when they investigate large-scale political institutions but also when they look at the power exercised in everyday life by individuals—including in the classroom. "The personal is political," an early feminist statement maintained, and the full range of student intellectual authority needs to be voiced.

The problem remains, however, that even in a world of equals women may not feel the authority to speak. This feeling that one lacks authority applies to teachers as well as students especially in diverse classrooms unless intersectionality is well explained and dif-ference processed. There are many women of great knowledge and experience who may claim to have a fear of being found to be a fraud. They believe that they lack the right to speak and that any-thing they have to say is not really worthy of being said. Students may discover their unworthiness, as do their teachers, who often feel that they, even though holding doctorates, are imposters. The imposter syndrome is extremely common among women in high positions. The idea they hold is that, as women, they should be domestic workers or housewives or hold other low positions in society or the economy. There is the hope that awareness of this shared sense of lacking legitimacy will help overcome it in order to build both classroom and community citizenship.

CONCLUSION

A major quest in today's world is for belonging and citizenship, which can mean different things according to location across the globe. Over the course of *Women's Studies: The Basics* we have seen that states of both the global South and global North institute structures and support behaviors that work against women's sense of belonging and their full citizenship. We see the Women's Studies classroom where civic skills can be built and civic consciousness raised. There, contentious issues are aired in an informed and safe way, so that students and teachers build and reinforce one another's capacities. There are many sharp disagreements among Women's Studies practitioners, all of them susceptible to a good airing. The status of feminism is also contentious and a good topic to debate. If the feeling of being inadequate or an imposter is prevalent, there is no better place to explore that feeling than the classroom. Those who are strengthened in the classroom will be armed with the attitudes and fortitude of the worthy citizen.

SUGGESTED READING

Ahmed, Sara (2012) *On Being Included: Racism and Diversity in Institutional Life.* Durham: Duke University Press.

Hawkesworth, Mary E. (2012) *Political Worlds of Women: Activism, Advocacy, and Governance in the Twenty-first Century.* Boulder, CO: Westview.

Jakobson, Janet R. and Pellegrini, Ann (2003) *Love the Sin: Sexual Regulation and the Limits of Religious Tolerance.* New York: New York University Press.

Mahmood, Saba (2005) *Politics of Piety: The Islamic Revival and the Feminist Subject.* Princeton, NJ: Princeton University Press.

Robinson, Catherine (1999) *Tradition and Liberation: The Hindu Tradition in the Indian Women's Movement.* New York: St. Martin's Press.

Salime, Zakia (2011) *Between Feminism and Islam: Human Rights and Sharia Law in Morocco*. Minneapolis, MN: University of Minnesota Press.

Scott, Joan Wallach (2007) *The Politics of the Veil*. Princeton, NJ: Princeton University Press.

Yuval-Davis, Nira (2011) *The Politics of Belonging: Intersectional Contestations*. London: Sage.

Yuval-Davis, Nira and Werbner, Pnina (eds.) (1999) *Women, Citizenship, and Difference*. New York: St. Martin's Press.

9

THE FUTURE OF WOMEN'S STUDIES IN OUR INFORMATION AGE

Given this activity and all the activity gathered over the past five decades, many question the need for Women's Studies today. Hasn't enough already changed to allow Women's Studies to disappear? Haven't we heard enough about women—the wage gap, the voting gap, their poverty, and the double shift? News of the constant violence against women becomes depressing or boring or we grow immune to it. It is normal, we say, all this evidence of women's abuse, so let's just get used to it. Besides that, women's situation seems to have improved dramatically. Today's students have not only seen women beside them in the classroom but active as television anchors or as authoritative commentators on issues of the day.

Have things really changed all that much? Women's Studies advocates say "no," adding that important information and new ways of thinking come forth every day. In this chapter we look at the pros and cons for continuing Women's Studies. We also look at some of the areas where Women's Studies pioneering is still in its infancy and where dramatic change continues to take place. Social and political questions affecting the status of women form an important part of our debate, and we evaluate the place of women in the economy. This is a place where you, the reader, have your own judgments to draw about the value of Women's Studies and its place in your society and the world. We ask you to decide whether Women's Studies still has a role to play.

WHY WOMEN'S STUDIES SHOULD END

In the university, there is a call for "enough" and the charge remains that Women's Studies is simply not up to standard. Isn't the study of women perverting scholarly values, as prominent British historian David Starkey asserted in 2009 when he criticized a television series about the wives of King Henry VIII? Researching queens is simply to focus on the trivial—clothing, furniture, and bodily functions. We aren't learning enough about the important men, Starkey proclaimed of the series' influence on culture more generally. Another criticism points to a still different issue: in US universities the number of women undergraduates exceeds the number of men—evidence of the special privileging of women and proof that equality and even women's dominance have been achieved. In fact, there is the complaint that the university is becoming degraded as an institution wherever men are in declining numbers. The presence of women has brought about an end to standards of rigor and excellence that had once been the pride of university life. The university is no longer about the muscular exercise of intelligence.

At the elementary school level in the United States, critics announce loudly that boys are being neglected and their confidence has declined because of the women's movement. Boys are becoming lethargic and sad. There is more talk of suicide among them online and among friends. The suggestion is that the entire educational system is cheating men, who are in crisis because of the attention given to women since the onset of second wave feminism. When they grow up, too much material about women in the curriculum holds men back not just intellectually but emotionally. The lack of critical thinking and high-level information because of material on women in the curriculum has slowed the pace men formerly kept as innovators and has even caused their discouragement and eventually brought about unemployment. In this view Women's Studies threatens the well-being of the world as a whole and should be abolished as quickly as possible.

There is also the well-worn accusation that students in Women's Studies are queers and lesbians. The university is sheltering perverts in Women's Studies classes and even empowering them to convert their peers to becoming lesbian or gay. Parents often worry that their children will not find jobs if they take a Women's Studies major or concentration, especially if they appear to be feminist. Among women there is the additional charge against Women's Studies that it *is* connected to feminism, especially that view of feminism as a uniformly man-hating set of principles and ideas. Stereotypes around the world additionally suggest that feminism is a Western ideology—an accusation that erases the fact that feminism has existed in many parts of the world since at least the late nineteenth century. Another charge is that all feminists, especially those in Europe and the United States, are racists and that those old-timers from the second wave remain so. Those who believe this maintain their distance, claiming to be enlightened and thus wanting nothing to do with the racist heritage so firmly ingrained in feminism. Still another grievance against Women's Studies as it is connected to feminism is that both are classist and elitist, involving only non-working, parasitical, and privileged women. This too is a common charge globally. Many people today thus erase the history of working-class women-centered activism whether in England, Nigeria, or South Korea—on which we have touched in this book. Others feel that the proliferation of theories in Women's Studies is another sign of elitism and classism, showing its lack of concern for the real problems of women around the world. In present-day India Dalit activists give an example of feminist classism. The upper-class Indian feminist, Dalit women charge, sees Dalits "as having only experience not intelligence" (Gandoli 2007:11). Based on these arguments, Women's Studies, like feminism, is not only no longer needed but also *needs* to go. Clearly there is much to think about when it comes to the future of Women's Studies.

POST-FEMINISM

Let us look at the alternatives to feminism and to Women's Studies. In Europe and the United States one of these is a complex of ideas and practices today clustered under the rubric "post-feminism." A different sense of women's place in the world shapes the attitudes of a generation of young women at the present who believe it is time to move into an era beyond feminism. They muster many arguments, some based on the "mission accomplished" scenario. Aren't women everywhere in the seats of power, in the workforce, and in the university, they ask? Is there any good reason to continue Women's Studies given all the change that has taken place? Their lives are good and fulfilling, many of these "post-feminists" tell us, ending the need for feminism. They produce many arguments against the continuation of Women's Studies, among them that the mainstreaming of knowledge about women has already occurred and that everything there is to know about women is in the curriculum from kindergarten through to university. (When second wave feminism first started many had the goal of mainstreaming.) In the late twentieth century women entered the top ranks of governmental power across the world and influenced growing, if unsteady and uneven, global prosperity. Indira Gandhi kept the momentum for a healthy independent India alive in the 1970s and early 1980s, while Corazon Aquino likewise is seen as advancing development as president of the Philippines. Across Latin America and Scandinavia women have come to power in even greater numbers, as they also have in the rest of Europe. Prime minister of the United Kingdom Margaret Thatcher in the 1980s and chancellor of Germany Angela Merkel in the twenty-first century shaped the economic future of the world in a variety of ways. In the twenty-first century, Merkel has been seen as perhaps the single most important person in determining the economic health of the world. These simple facts suggest that Women's Studies has done its job.

A final post-feminist argument is that throughout their young years newly adult women will have had no road blocks to getting contraception or other reproductive counseling. The world may have left undisturbed their growth into mature, sexual people of whatever sexual orientation. There are many personal stories to support this rejection of the feminist agenda including Women's Studies. For some the situation of women and equality simply goes without saying: "In college, I was introduced academically to feminism as the belief in equal rights and opportunities for both sexes. Well that's just American, I thought" (Goudreau 2011). No Women's Studies needed. For others, Women's Studies conjured up the image of screaming feminists: "negative and ugly and inappropriate," as CNN newsreader Soledad O'Brien called the earlier generation of activists for women's rights (Goudreau 2011). Women's Studies also looks as if it has a race and class bias to some, which it did at the beginning. Still others have moved on to present post-feminism as a set of ideas and behaviors in the media and on the web where ordinary women are shown to be empowered. It is this proliferation of ideas composing post-feminism that we want to explore in more detail.

Important in making their decision to embrace the idea of post-feminism is the fact that they themselves have good jobs and have not experienced overt discrimination. They may have gone to elite schools and succeeded in their studies without facing sexual harassment or difficulties in navigating the search for jobs or male mentors. Unlike first and second wave feminists in the West, who they say hated men, contemporary women around the world bond with men, either as comrades in suffering oppression as the African activist stated in Chapter 4, or as good pals in the "gender-enlightened" workforce as depicted increasingly in the media since early in the 1980s. Since the rise of second wave feminism, the young may also have seen women's growing political sophistication, as they take up leadership positions in local and district governments around the world. They have watched or heard of feminists meeting globally in successful, well-publicized congresses from the 1970s to 1995; these congresses have drawn up plans to make women's future brighter. In fact, the difference between women's political participation before World War II and today is striking. Additionally, women's health has improved, often leading them to greater achievement than in the past. One older male interviewee on a global news program, when asked to identify the biggest change over his lifetime, responded that it was the appearance of women in politics, the economy, and intellectual life. Women were in public life in ways he had never imagined would happen. Any student reading this will have had women as teachers not just in primary school but in the universities; they will have consulted women medical doctors, and perhaps even women lawyers; they will have watched women newsreaders on television or women performers in a variety of venues. They know that there are women millionaires and even some women billionaires. Indeed it looks as if there has been dramatic change, making this age ripe for post-feminism because there are no more impediments to their happiness, wealth, and power.

This survey of opinions shows post-feminists as pointing optimistically to the future and heralding the new possibilities for women's power and their presence on the world stage. It is about achievement, not oppression, and lays out the new ways in which post-feminists envision their place in the world. Post-feminism in this sense of the word is not a wholesale rejection of feminism but instead succeeds it as part of a progression. Post-feminism is only "post," the argument goes, because of the new conditions created by mass consumerism, the mass media, and the digital revolution. These developments constitute the evidence that allows young women to see the world as entirely different for them in positive ways, as the dislocations of the industrial revolution and colonization formed the conditions for the first wave and globalization and post-colonialism for the second.

We see post-feminists constantly represented in the media. For one thing, their lives are made up of friendships with other women and the enjoyment of their company. This enjoyment is based on all kinds of discussions including those on sex, clothing, troubles at work, and problems with partners or other loved ones. For another, post-feminists can flaunt their sexuality and even be sexually aggressive. They can be happy in their experimentation as sexual beings or in their work lives because little holds them back in their expression of agency. Finally, cross-racial friendships flourish, as postfeminists embrace diversity. Post-feminism, then, is about affirmation.

Post-feminists are pathfinders and innovators, adopting and being adopted by technology of which earlier feminists had no idea (the South Asian writer Rokeya Sakhawat Hossain imagined the successes of high-tech women more than a hundred years ago, however). Post-feminists can even jettison their gender online or make their female identities link with those in distant cultures. New identities can include that of master technician, or with the help of medicine embrace a host of normative or non-normative embodied selves. They trouble the boundaries of gender while simultaneously acknowledging that these exist and can be constraining.

Critics find much in post-feminism to dislike and call it valueless, producing commodity-driven lives. Post-feminists have an eye on their own success and satisfactions. Instead of joining together for collective action and social improvement, they concentrate on sexual satisfaction and owning material goods with designer labels.

They are thus apolitical and fail in their duties as citizens to participate responsibly in public life. Defenders, however, note that post-feminists are disposed to seeing the positive in their lives and making the positive apparent to the world. Organized movements attacking "problems" only see the negative and are, more importantly, outmoded. In the digital age, if the self is positively attuned to the world, communication can create political change in minutes and in serious cases can mobilize tens of thousands virtually in an instant. Witness the Arab Spring. Witness the immediate calling to order of protestors to any harms done to women during such events.

HAS THE WORLD REALLY CHANGED ALL THAT MUCH?

Let's now look at the arguments for Women's Studies, some of them in fact pointing to lingering negative conditions for women and conditions in need of further study. In contrast to post-feminists and other critics, many hold the belief that Women's Studies has just begun to look at persistent problems in society—problems that have not changed for millennia. For example, no one has solved the mystery of patriarchy or explored it in a convincing historical fashion that takes into account patriarchy's global grip. Who understands why the world's most powerful countries—the United States, China, and Russia—are relentlessly patriarchal? Any newscast of high political moments shows these three countries as dominated exclusively by men over the past century and, in the case of the United States, over its entire history. Violence against women persists and even appears to be on the increase, while capitalist structures of industry and finance show women making few if any gains. Indeed, as we have shown in this book, women make up the vast pool of the impoverished across the globe and their lives show little basis for post-feminist optimism.

Being able to stamp the Women's Studies agenda as complete would entail an understanding as to how and why it is that men have ruled women for most of human history right down to the present, especially in those countries that are the wealthiest and most powerful. Women's Studies scholarship would also have witnessed the righting of the many and vast injustices that exist, when in fact many scholars see those injustices as alive and well in rich and poor countries alike. We believe, alongside the black women theorists of Chapter 6, that there is much more to do simply to discover why black women and women of color are seen as far less valuable— monetarily, politically, intellectually, and physically—than whites. Why do all women earn less money? Why are they the ones who can be beaten and abused without consequence? Why are they seen as stupid politically and in most other ways so that they are not to hold important jobs or serve as major cultural leaders? Or, to put it another way, why are men seen as smarter, more valuable, and deserving of more money and privilege than women? If men are better in every way than women, it remains to find out why. More than that, we need to have our very selves and our studies shaken to the core and disturbed by the degradation we in Women's Studies confront not only of women but of humans in general, both in today's world and in the past. Clearly there is much more study necessary to confront injustice from an informed and engaged position in order to continue answering these questions.

BURNING ISSUES THAT REMAIN

The evidence suggests that Women's Studies has hardly begun to find answers to the burning questions of the inequality of the sexes and the life-crushing harm of sexism, racism, homophobia, and other forms of hatred. It is Women's Studies that helped begin the process of bringing these injustices into focus as a group. Nor has information to date had an effect on conditions such as the wage gap and the higher value placed on men. Historian Judith Bennett in a recent study shows that women's wages as a percentage of men's remain what they were in the Middle Ages, at 70 to 75 percent of men's in the best conditions. In 2011 in the United States the figure was 78 percent of men's wages and declining. Globally even women in privileged jobs such as the university are still dominant in the lower posts, obtain positions of distinction less often, and are less well paid. Bennett suggests that Women's Studies has been too focused on minute evidence of change—say from one year to another. From her longer-term vantage point continuity of conditions over the centuries is the norm when it comes to women's income. The gap is the same as it was one thousand years ago! Nothing, in her view, has in fact changed when it comes down to the crucial question of women's economic well-being.

Violence against women also continues, and is a huge social and political problem in many parts of the world: rape, genocide, and other forms of political violence specifically target women. Amidst this, "saving women" is an international political mantra used to justify interventions of many sorts, but the situation has hardly been remedied. As mentioned often throughout this book, the poverty of women and children is a global disgrace and a threat to the human race as a whole. How can society be healthy and beautiful as post-feminists declare it to be, when violence toward half of humanity is rarely felt as troubling? These and other facts show that there is perhaps an overwhelming argument for the continuation of Women's Studies to investigate such conditions as the rising tide of women as war booty and war victims; the rising level of women's poverty around the world and of domestic abuse and violence towards women and girls; women's higher levels of illiteracy; and the intersectionality of all these conditions. We need perhaps to look at continuity over time in our studies or to dig back to find the origins, if there are any, of the idea that men deserve more than women in terms of safety from violence, food and shelter, and equality of income and opportunity. Can we find our answers in the newly-developed theories and feminist methods of Women's Studies that are just being born? Let's deploy all of them to find solutions and to challenge one another to research further.

Were the Women's Studies mission finished, there would be not only an understanding of patriarchy but its eradication. Had the Women's Studies agenda been completed, it would have come up with solutions to the gross abuse of women that persists and some say is accelerating in our own time. Doesn't society need Women's Studies to push further to end the problem of violence against women? Doesn't the situation deserve more than the four decades of Women's Studies' existences? Have scientists stopped working to cure cancer because they have been at it for four and more decades? The continuation of Women's Studies seems especially urgent given the current and past use of rape as a political and military tool and the persistence of violence against women in all strata of society. Top politicians around the world rule with impunity even as they abuse prostitutes, the women in their families, and even complete strangers. It is fine for them to display misogyny in their published remarks and to behave in an even worse manner to women around them. Beyond that and many other lingering topics for research, the world is changing rapidly before our eyes, bringing with it further issues of concern to women, including their place within the ever-changing life of the planet and in virtual culture. Women's place in this digital age is evolving and remains to be understood.

There also remain many other complicated problems to research and solve that involve women and gender. We might even study why there is this chorus of complaint against the existence of Women's Studies. Isn't this evidence enough that the historic campaign against women's equality exists? Should not Women's Studies research examine this issue too? We conclude this presentation of the basics in Women's Studies with a review of where Women's Studies began, where it has traveled, and where it is located in the twenty-first century not only in terms of scholarship but also in regard to its relevance to lived experience.

FLOWS, FLUX, AND NOMADS

If we think that the study of women began centuries ago and that organized movements for women's rights are some two centuries old, we might consider what has changed in our own twenty-first century. To some extent Women's Studies began such consideration long ago in looking at the gendering of globalization. People are mobile these days as never before, unsettled and even nomadic. They have artificial body parts and mechanical appendages such as iPods and iPhones and, in an increasingly large number of cases, virtual existences that seem to be disembodied. The strong lines of the self that shaped feminist and Women's Studies' thought for decades seems to be disappearing, leading in some cases to a weakening of older forms of feminism as embodied and theoretical ways of acting and thinking in sturdy feminist groups. Let's look at some of these new conditions affecting the content and status of Women's Studies in greater depth in order to see what the agenda for Women's Studies might look like at present and in the future.

The world is in flux, we are told. More to the point, change and movement are apparent everywhere as people migrate for better health care in Africa, for high-tech jobs from Asia, for temporary employment as maids and nurses from North Africa and Latin America, and for personal freedoms and safety from many other parts of the world. We migrate internally from rural to urban areas and from south to north and vice versa. Women in particular are migrants from areas of civil war, genocide, and personal violence to safer regions of the world. Our flux is physical, making the term "nomad" a physical and very palpable one. "The definition of a person's identity takes place in between nature–technology, male–female, black–white, in the spaces that flow and connect in between," Dutch theorist Rosi Braidotti writes. "We live in permanent processes of transition, hybridization and nomadization and these in-between states and stages defy the established modes of theoretical representation" (Braidotti 2002: 2). Many agree with Braidotti that our current situation is one that hardly crossed the minds of Women's Studies' founders and that demands rethinking.

Thus one lesson from Women's Studies over the past 40 years is that our modern condition is far more complex than anyone had imagined and that ongoing change is making all of us in between old and new selves and old assigned identities and newer, more fluid ones. We are always moving and transitioning—flowing and in flux. Moreover, Women's Studies shows how indeterminate gender identities can be even as the treatment of those assigned certain identities—including race, ethnicity, class, and gender—is discriminatory because identity is said to be clear and obvious. Having brought the complexity and fluidity of identity to light, Women's Studies aims to examine from a variety of perspectives what can be called a "nomadic" because always fluid self.

These are not, as some complain, simply fancy ways of talking. They indicate a changing reality with actual consequences for people's lives whether they be among the millions of the world's migrants or undergoing sex-reassignment surgery. As multinational corporations constantly make new demands on global workers, their work lives too are in a perpetual state of flux. Indeed, it is estimated that many of the world's women move from job to job— and often from place to place. In economically developed countries workers also move from occupation to occupation. Thus, work identities, like identity that comes from a nation or locality, are also in a state of flux. Indeed, representations of women change as well, depending on class, political needs, and the state of the advertising or fashion worlds. One is not born but made a woman, the author Simone de Beauvoir wrote more than 60 years ago. The terms of that "making" are far more fluid than what they had been in de Beauvoir's time, however, and perhaps different from what feminists had in mind only four decades ago.

OUR VIRTUAL SELVES AND THE INTERNET SOLUTION

Another ingredient of that fluidity comes from the digital revolution that now allows for disembodied identities in cyberspace. Technology has also enabled women's identities to be changeable, differently organized, or voluntarily hidden from the gender order itself. It's not only that women have a new technology that they can master; women have mastered whatever the prevailing technology is for millennia. Careers that might once have been closed to them are now open and women have excelled at launching web-based businesses often with far less gender prejudice. The fact is that women can master a technology far more enabling than its predecessors.

For example, Muslim women can and do organize themselves across the internet space, listing their points of advocacy, sharing information, organizing campaigns on their own and others' behalf, and generally making themselves a vital global presence. Decades ago, French lesbians used the first incarnation of the World Wide Web to make connections in a world that was hostile to them. Information about women's health, finance, political role, and historical past has all been more widely broadcast and more readily available than ever before. Because of the internet it is somewhat easier to track predators of women. Support groups for women with cancer and other diseases function via the web as does fund-raising for myriad women's causes.

The fact is that women are creating their own forms of activism and knowledge production that supplements and contributes another dimension to Women's Studies. There are now websites and blogs that call themselves "Girrrl," and "Jezebel"; new names have been coined or revived such as "mujerista" and "womanist." This is the post-feminist "upside" to the new technology, but as we are ever made aware our digital age is full of exploitation precisely because of this technology and its use by powerful people at points very distant from our own. They too may have many advantages in being disembodied and never accountable. Paradoxes abound in considering the gender implications; however, the adventuresome spirit of Women's Studies research, as we have seen, thrives on dealing with complexity and contradiction.

WE ARE CYBORGS: BEYOND THE HUMAN-CENTERED WORLD: THE POST-HUMAN

Over its brief lifespan Women's Studies scholars have also come to critique the human-centered world from a variety of perspectives and with the result of a variety of insights. From the beginning volleys in Women's Studies scholarship, charges have arisen that the gendered equation of man the manipulator of nature and nature as a dominated woman has led us on the path to disaster. In our current day, we see those disasters everywhere, from explosions in nuclear facilities to the state of our own solar system. Hubris, as it emerges from standard gendered norms, has wreaked havoc on the world in which we live, putting the entire planet at great risk—risk that we see materializing all around us. Women's Studies has called for a less human-centered vision of our existence so that life in all its multiple forms can endure.

One proposed innovation is a re-envisioning of the human and the post-human. An example of this re-envisioning comes from Donna Haraway, who proposes that humans have become cyborgs—that is, beings who have been transformed by the incorporation of machines into their existence. This may include dependence on microwaves and automobiles and a more intimate dependence on pacemakers, hearing aids, and other mechanisms implanted in the body. The implications of human relationship to machines, however, can be part of the hubris mentioned above, but it should also lead to new formulations of the human as more situated in a broad context of existence and more embedded in relationships to the non-human world. In other words, the recognition of cyborgism should engender questioning about identities and even a realization that we are no longer the self-contained and privileged beings on which so much of politics, the social order (including gender), economies, and environments have depended.

To the contrary, a lot of thinking is currently occurring in Women's Studies—still with a long way to go—to understand what our "post-human" condition means for the existence of what we once called individuals, localities, the non-human world, and the planet. Are cells the common denominator of post-human existence rather than individual human selves? Are we still the whole human individual traditionally seen as endowed with human rights because of our autonomy and wholeness? Post-human theories such as Haraway's suggest that in fact our lives are intertwined with those of machines, with the implication that we need to analyze gender not in terms of the human condition but in terms of the post-human condition. We are enmeshed in systems of signs, languages, and influences that signal both our dependency and the permeability of what was once seen as an independent human race. Women's Studies has led the way in considering the meaning of post-humanism as it extends to women and beyond, both now and in the future.

OUR PLACE IN THE ANIMAL KINGDOM

As we saw in the development of queer theory, new findings on the lives of animals has given Women's Studies much food for thought. In showing that sexuality, reproduction, and social relations are variable in the animal world, it has given new, if perhaps disconcerting answers to one of the original questions in Women's Studies: What is a woman? Simultaneously, studies of animal life are among the influences that have led Women's Studies researchers to consider human life in the continuum of life on the planet more generally. Animal Studies is a growing field within Women's Studies and new connections are being explored.

Considering the overall conservatism of biological studies when it came to ideas about women, this is perhaps a surprising turn of events. Indeed, animal epithets have often been applied to women, while animal scientists often fail to use insights from Women's and Gender Studies in their work. On the side of Women's Studies, some would like to erase from women's nature their bodily home, which has too often been seen as lacking in brain power while overactive in sexual and reproductive power—like animals. Part of women's status as the "other" to men is precisely the female body she shares with animals.

At this point, there opens a connection to what is newly called "Critical Animal Studies," and that is a shared, if different, kind of oppression such as the degradation that women have experienced and that animals face in relation to humans who at every turn flaunt their superiority. All the while focusing on animals, the goal of Critical Animal Studies is similar to that of Women's Studies: to end oppression. The institution seen as instrumental in that oppression is capitalism in the eyes of many proponents of Critical Animal Studies, and some Women's Studies activists target that same oppression. Other shared tactics are the unpacking of representations to demonstrate how literature, the arts, and other media use animals as descriptors of menace, devoted love, loyalty, or brutality. Because Women's Studies has helped us understand the current tendency to demonize others or to develop negative stereotypes of those who are different, it continues to open up scholarly investigations of the animal world. It charts concepts of gender, sexuality, identity, and intersectionality and continues to integrate and innovate because of its interdisciplinarity and openness.

CONCLUSION

Women's Studies, bringing together both old and new disciplines, has come to raise many important questions about individuals, societies, and our cosmos. Some in Women's Studies now contest all these former categories of research; others forge new understandings and take us into the twenty-first century armed with new thinking skills and many new facts. Some of these new facts concern the perpetuation into our present day of economic discrimination and violence against women. In other words, new facts deal with longstanding problems of the seemingly perpetual perceived inferiority of women. Other new facts concern our perhaps indeterminate identities and the greater complexity of changes in our lifetimes. Although some people miss the ferment of the early days of Women's Studies, others find that ferment still active and even accelerating. Just the few new points of concern mentioned in this chapter—Animal Studies, cyborgs and technology, our nomadic condition, and the promise and perils of globalization—give us plenty to ponder in terms of women and gender. We still have not integrated all the theories stemming from the many perspectives of

Women's Studies into our individual practices nor into our thinking about the world. From these advances and insights we draw the conclusion not that the time has come to abandon Women's Studies but rather that it is time to advance its operations and recharge out thinking. We need to enhance Women's Studies' place in schools and universities and in our everyday lives. Women's Studies continues to offer plenty to do, both now and in the future.

SUGGESTED READING

Braidotti, Rosi (2002) *Metamorphoses: Towards a Materialist Theory of Becoming*. Cambridge: Polity.

Gandoli, Geetanjali (2007) *Indian Feminisms: Law, Patriarchies and Violence in India*. Aldershot: Ashgate.

Genz, Stephanie and Bravon, Benjamin A. (2009) *Postfeminism: Cultural Texts and Theories*. Edinburgh: University of Edinburgh Press.

Goudreau, Jenna (2011) *Who's Afraid of Post-Feminism? What It Means To Be A Feminist Today*, Forbes. Online. Available HTTP: <http://www.forbes.com/sites/jennagoudreau/2011/12/13/afraid-of-post-feminism-means-feminist-today-gloria-steinem-jane-fonda-ursula-burns> (accessed 16 June 2012)

Halberstam, Judith and Livingston, Ira (eds.) (1995) *Post-human Bodies*. Bloomington, IN: Indiana University Press.

Haraway, Donna J. (2004) *The Haraway Reader*. London: Routledge.

Kirkup, Gill (2000) *The Gendered Cyborg: A Reader*. London: Routledge.

Moghadam, Valentine (2005) *Globalizing Woman: Transnational Feminist Networks*. Baltimore, MD: Johns Hopkins University Press.

Ng, Cecilia and Mitter, Swasti (2005) *Gender and the Digital Economy: Perspectives from the Developing World*. New Delhi: Sage.

Wallach Scott, Joan (ed.) (2008) *Women's Studies on the Edge*. Durham: Duke University Press.

Weil, Kari (2012) *Thinking Animals: Why Animal Studies Now?* New York: Columbia University Press.

Wiegman, Robyn (ed.) (2002) *Women's Studies on Its Own*. Durham: Duke University Press.

INDEX

ROUTLEDGE

Gender in *The Key Concepts*

Gender: The Key Concepts

Mary Evans, London School of Economics and
Carolyn Williams, London School of Economics

This invaluable volume provides an overview of 37 terms, theories and concepts
frequently used in gender studies which those studying the subject can find
difficult to grasp. Each entry provides a critical definition of the concept, examining
the background to the idea, its usage and the major figures associated with the
term. Taking a truly interdisciplinary and global view of gender studies, concepts
covered include:

- Agency
- Diaspora
- Heteronormativity
- Subjectivity
- Performativity
- Class
- Feminist Politics
- Body
- Gender identity
- Reflexivity.

With cross referencing and further reading provided throughout the text, *Gender:
The Key Concepts* unweaves the relationships between different aspects of the
field defined as gender studies, and is essential for all those studying gender in
interdisciplinary contexts as undergraduates, postgraduates and beyond.

October 2012 – 280 pages
Pb: 978-0-415-66962-7| Hb: 978-0-415-66961-0

For more information and to order a copy visit
http://www.routledge.com/books/details/9780415669627/

Available from all good bookshops

http://www.routledge.com/books/series/B/

Research Methods in *The Basics*

Research Methods: The Basics

Nicholas Walliman, Oxford Brookes University

Research Methods: The Basics is an accessible, user-friendly introduction to the different aspects of research theory, methods and practice. Structured in two parts, the first covering the nature of knowledge and the reasons for research, and the second the specific methods used to carry out effective research, this book covers:

- structuring and planning a research project
- the ethical issues involved in research
- different types of data and how they are measured
- collecting and analyzing data in order to draw sound conclusions
- devising a research proposal and writing up the research.

Complete with a glossary of key terms and guides to further reading, this book is an essential text for anyone coming to research for the first time, and is widely relevant across the social sciences and humanities.

November 2010 – 194 pages
Pb: 978-0-415-48994-2| Hb: 978-0-415-48991-1

For more information and to order a copy visit
http://www.routledge.com/books/details/9780415489942/

Available from all good bookshops

Sociology in *The Basics*

Sociology: The Basics

Ken Plummer, University of Essex

A lively, accessible and comprehensive introduction to the diverse ways of thinking about social life, *Sociology: The Basics* examines:

- the scope, history and purpose of sociology
- ways of understanding 'the social'
- the state of the world we live in today
- suffering and social inequalities
- key tools for researching and thinking about 'the social'
- the impact of new technologies.

The reader is encouraged to think critically about the structures, meanings, histories and cultures found in the rapidly changing world we live in. With tasks to stimulate the sociological mind and suggestions for further reading both within the text and on an accompanying webpage, this book is essential reading for all those studying sociology, and those with an interest in how the modern world works.

June 2010 – 256 pages
Pb: 978-0-415-47206-7 | Hb: 978-0-415-47205-0

For more information and to order a copy visit
http://www.routledge.com/books/details/9780415472067/

Available from all good bookshops

Wollstonecraft in *Routledge Guides to the Great Books*

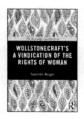

The Routledge Guidebook to Wollstonecraft's A Vindication of the Rights of Woman

Sandrine Berges,
Bilkent University, Turkey

Mary Wollstonecraft was one of the greatest philosophers and writers of the eighteenth century. During her brief career she wrote novels, treatises, a travel narrative, a history of the French Revolution, a conduct book, and a children's book. Her most celebrated and widely-read work is *A Vindication of the Rights of Woman*. This Guidebook introduces:

- Wollstonecraft's life and the background to *A Vindication of the Rights of Woman*
- The ideas and text of *A Vindication of the Rights of Woman*
- Wollstonecraft's enduring influence in philosophy and our contemporary intellectual life.

It is ideal for anyone coming to Wollstonecraft's classic text for the first time and anyone interested in the origins of feminist thought.

February 2013 – 272 pages
Pb: 978-0-415-67414-0 | Hb: 978-0-415-67415-7